THE BIG BOO

2 BOOKS

OVER 300 ESSENTIAL PHRASES

ORBIS LANGUAGE CENTER

Book 1:

101 Spanish Phrases You Won't Learn in School

The Key to Sounding Like a Native Speaker: Idioms & Popular Phrases You Don't Learn from Textbooks

Introduction:

Thank you for purchasing this book and congratulations on taking the next step in your language education. You are far ahead of most people because you're willing to take your education into your own hands in ways like purchasing this book.

So you've learned the basics in Spanish Class. You know how to say, "¿Cómo estás?" or "¿Dónde está el baño?" or "¿Cuantos años tienes?" but how do you take it to the next level?

Discover one of the most important yet often one of the most overlooked aspects of a language: idioms and popular phrases in common use. Think about how in English, so much of what we say is full of expressions and figures of speech and idioms.

We say things like: "dime a dozen," or "beat around the bush," "cutting corners," "speak of the devil," etc. Plus, there is so much slang and so many phrases in popular use especially with young people: "To have a crush on someone," "I'm all set," "I'm down for that," etc. Plus there are so many slang words we use that have other meanings in popular use like: "cool," or "sick" or "lame" etc. This is the same if not even more common in the Spanish language.

If you want to be able to understand people and speak comfortably, you will find it almost impossible without a healthy knowledge of popular idioms, words, and phrases used by native Spanish Speakers.

This book will teach you 101 of the most popular Spanish Idioms and phrases that take you far beyond the basics you may have learned in school.

You will learn:

- The English and Spanish version of the idiom/phrase
- The explanation of how to use this idiom or phrase in common speech and when is an appropriate time to use it
- Examples of casual dialogue in both Spanish and English to show you the context of how this phrase is used
- You can practice repeating each phrase to help commit it to memory and work through the pronunciation

Now you can unlock an entire new level of ability and gain the street-knowledge and confidence you need to have real conversations in Spanish.

So, without delay, let's start learning 101 Spanish Phrases You Won't Learn in School. We will start with some more basic phrases that provide you with a different, less formal and more conversational way of saying some things you may have learned, then we will progress to more advanced phrases that will be sure to impress anyone you come in contact with.

1) How've you been?

En Español: ¿Cómo te ha ido?

En Inglés: How've You Been?

This is useful especially if you're speaking to someone you've met before or someone you have an ongoing relationship with. Especially if cómo estas (How are you?) feels too formal or awkward. It's a more casual way of inquiring about someone.

Dialogue:

Margarita: ¡Hola Pedro!

(Hi, Pedro!)

Pedro: ¡Hola Margarita! ¿Cómo te ha ido?

(Hi Margarita! How have you been?)

Now Practice: ¿Cómo te ha ido?

Repeat 3 times aloud, slowly

---

2) What's up?

En Español: ¿Qué tal?

En Inglés: What's up?

Context:

This is a very typical thing to say after the initial greeting with someone. But it's more of a casual phrase so don't use it in a formal situation.

Dialogue:

Margarita: ¡Hola Pedro!

(Hi, Pedro!)

Pedro: ¡Hola Margarita! ¿Qué tal?

Hi Margarita! What's up?

Now Practice: Qué Tal

Repeat 3 times aloud, slowly

---

3) Sorry?

En Español: ¿Disculpe?

En Inglés: Sorry?

Context:

You use this phrase if you didn't hear someone when they were speaking to you and you need them to repeat it. In English we would say, "I'm Sorry?" In Spanish they say, "Disculpe."

Dialogue:

Margarita: ¿Qué quieres hacer hoy, Pedro?

(What would you like to do today, Pedro?)

Pedro: ¿Disculpe?

(Sorry?)

Now Practice: Disculpe

Repeat 3 times aloud, slowly

4) No problem!

En Español: ¡Sin problema!

En Inglés: No problem!

Context:

This is a friendlier more casual response to "Gracias" (Thank you in English). Normally you learn to say "de nada." But often it might be better to say "Sin Problema." This literally translates to: without a problem. Use this especially in informal situations.

Dialogue:

Margarita: Gracias, Pedro para ayudarme con este problema.

(Thank you, Pedro, for helping me with this problem.)

Pedro: ¡Sin problema, Margarita!

(No Problem Margarita!)

Now Practice: ¡Sin problema!

Repeat 3 times aloud, slowly

5) I have no idea

En Español: No tengo ni idea

En Inglés: I have no idea

Context:

You can use this instead of "No se" (I don't know). It's a bit more sophisticated and more extreme than "no se." It can come off as a bit rude in the wrong situation so only use it with people you know or in the appropriate situation. You can always preface or finish it with "lo siento" (I'm sorry).

Dialogue:

Margarita: A qué hora termina este clase?

What time does this class end?

Pedro: No tengo ni idea.

(I have no idea)

Now Practice: No tengo ni idea

Repeat 3 times aloud, slowly

---

6) Have fun!

En Español: ¡Diviértete!

En Inglés: Have fun!

Context:

Use this the same you would the English phrase. This is actually a command. You are telling someone you hope they have fun or wishing them well. This is typically said in farewell to someone especially if they are departing to go do something or go on a trip for example.

Dialogue:

Margarita: ¿A dónde vas hoy, Pedro?

(Where are you going today, Pedro?)

Pedro: Voy a la playa con mi familia.

(I am going to the beach with my family).

Margarita: Ahh ¡Diviértete!

(Ahh Have fun!)

Now Practice: ¡Diviértete!

Repeat 3 times aloud, slowly

---

7) See you

En Español: Nos Vemos

En Inglés: See you

Context:

Use this as a less formal goodbye. In English it would be like saying "see ya" or "see ya later." You'd say this to someone you see regularly but you're not completely sure when you will see them next so it's more of just a vague: "see you…"

Dialogue:

Margarita: Necesito irme a casa ahora. Adios Pedro.

(I need to go home now. Goodbye Pedro)

Pedro: Nos Vemos, Margarita.

(See you Margarita)

Now Practice: Nos Vemos

Repeat 3 times aloud, slowly

---

8) Should we go for a drink?

En Español: ¿Vamos a tomar una copa?

In English: Shall we go for a drink?

Context:

This literally translates to "Are we going to take a cup?" but it means the same thing we mean when we say "do you want to get a drink?" or "shall we go for a drink?" This is a useful phrase especially when making new friends and acquaintances. It's a casual friendly way of indicating that you'd like to get to know the person better.

Dialogue:

Margarita: ¡Finalmente! Estoy terminado con mi trabajo.

(Finally! I'm done with my work.)

Pedro: ¡Bueno! ¿Qué vas a hacer ahora?

(Great! What are you going to do now?)

Margarita: Nada mucho. ¿Vamos a tomar una copa?

Now Practice: ¿Vamos a tomar una copa?

Repeat 3 times aloud, slowly

9) Don't worry about it

En Español: No pasa nada

En Inglés: Don't worry about it

Context:

You can use this phrase in a variety of circumstances. It's a familiar phrase that you should use with people you already know or in casual situations. For instance if someone apologizes about something trivial, for example: "Sorry I'm late." You can say "No pasa nada."

Dialogue:

Margarita: Todavía puedes ir al cine conmigo?

(Can you still go to the movies with me?)

Pedro: Lo siento, Margarita, no lo puedo. Me olvide que necesito trabajar hoy.

(I'm sorry Margarita I can't. I forgot I have to work today).

Margarita: Ah esta bien. No pasa nada.

(It's okay. Don't worry about it.)

Now Practice: No pasa nada.

Repeat 3 times aloud, slowly

---

10) I'll order the...

En Español: Me pones un...

En Inglés: I'll order the...

Context:

This is the most common way of ordering something at any restaurant pub or bar. People do not say: Puedo tener (Can I have) and they usually don't say "voy a ordenar" (I am going to order). The most common way of ordering is "Me pones un..." and then name whatever it is you're ordering. It may sound awkward to an English speaker because it translates to "put me a..." but this is actually the correct way to order.

Dialogue:

Margarita: Pedro es tu turno a ordenar.

(Pedro it's your turn to order).

Pedro: Vale. Me pones una hamburguesa sin queso con las fritas.

(Ok. I'll order the hamburger without cheese with fries).

Now Practice: Me pones un...

Repeat 3 times aloud, slowly

---

11) We're hanging out.

En Español: Aquí estamos

In English: We're hanging out/chilling

Context:

Although this directly translates to: We are here, it's usually an appropriate response if your friend asks you what's up or what you are doing. "We're just hanging out." It's not always the correct response but it's better than "Nada." Or "Nada mucho."

Dialogue:

Margarita: ¿Qué están haciendo tú y tu hermano?

(What are you and your brother doing?)

Pedro: Aquí estamos

(We're just hanging out.)

Margarita: Vale. ¿Puedo unirme a ustedes?

(Okay. Can I join you?)

Now Practice: Aquí Estamos.

Repeat 3 times aloud, slowly

---

12) Are you kidding me?/Are you pulling my leg?

En Español: Me estas tomando el pelo

In English: to pull someone's leg

Context:

This is Spanish phrase that directly translates to "take the hair." It's the same as the English phrase "to pull someone's leg." And it means I'm joking. Or I'm teasing you. Basically you say it when you tell someone something that isn't true to be funny. Or vice versa if they are telling you something and you think they're kidding, you can say "Me estas tomando el pelo."

Dialogue:

Margarita: ¿Tienes una novia?

(Do you have a girlfriend?)

Pedro: Si. Mi gato es mi novia.

(Yes, my cat is my girlfriend).

Margarita: Me estas tomando el pelo.

(You are pulling my leg.)

Now Practice: Me estas tomando el pelo.

Repeat 3 times aloud, slowly

---

13) A piece of advice…

En Español: Un buen consejo

En Inglés: a piece of advice…

Context:

You use this phrase when you want to offer some advice to someone. You can structure it at the beginning or the end of the sentence. Typically you'd only use this phrase with people you already know well or are already familiar with.

Dialogue:

Margarita: ¿Cómo fue el examen, Pedro?

(How was the text, Pedro?)

Pedro: Fue muy difícil. Un buen consejo: debes estudiar mucho.

(It was very difficult. A piece of advice: you should study a lot.)

Margarita: Ahora estoy nervioso.

(Now I'm nervous).

Now Practice: Un buen consejo…

Repeat 3 times aloud, slowly

---

14) A piece of cake

En Español: pan comido

En Inglés: Piece of cake

Context:

Much like the English phrase "it was a piece of cake," which means something was very easy or much easier than expected, the spanish phrase "pan comido" can be used in the same way. Fue pan comido. (It was a piece of cake.)

Dialogue:

Margarita: Acabo de terminar el primer día de mi nuevo trabajo.

(I just finished the first day of my new job.)

Pedro: ¿Cómo fue?

(How was it?)

Margarita: Va a ser pan comido.

(It's going to be a piece of cake.)

Now Practice: pan comido.

Repeat 3 times aloud, slowly

15) None of your business

En Español: No es cosa tuya

En Inglés: None of your business

Context:

Hopefully you won't have too much occasion to say this phrase. Of course you should only use it with friends or people you know well. Hopefully just as a joke or in good fun. Spanish speakers can be very sarcastic at times so it's good to know this phrase in case they use it on you as a joke.

Dialogue:

Pedro: ¿Cuánto dinero ganas en tu trabajo?

(How much money do you make?)

Margarita: No es cosa tuya.

(None of your business.)

Pedro: Jajajajaja

(hahahahah)

Now Practice: No es cosa tuya.

Repeat 3 times aloud, slowly

---

16) It will be okay

En Español: Saldrá bien

En Inglés: It will be okay

Context:

This is a good way of responding to someone if they tell you about a problem they're having. It's basically the future form of Esta bien.

Dialogue:

Margarita: Pienso que mi jefe me odia.

(I think my boss hates me.)

Pedro: ¿Por qué piensas esto?

(Why do you think this?)

Margarita: El nunca recuerda mi nombre.

(He never remembers my name.)

Pedro: El probablemente solo está ocupado. Saldrá bien.

(He is probably just busy. It will be okay.)

Now Practice: Saldrá bien.

Repeat 3 times aloud, slowly

---

17) To be in a bad mood

En Español: Tener un humor de perros

En Inglés: To be in a bad mood

Context:

This directly translates to "to have a mood of dogs." In English sometimes we say "you've had a dog day." Or You're sick as a dog. In Spanish they say the "mood of a dog" for "a bad mood." You will probably only use this in casual situations. You will impress people with your knowledge of the Spanish language.

Dialogue:

Margarita: ¿Qué pasa Pedro?

(What's wrong, Pedro?)

Pedro: Tengo un humor de perros.

(I'm in a bad mood)

Now Practice: Tener un humor de perros

Repeat 3 times aloud, slowly

---

18) To be angry with someone

En Español: Estar enojado con alguien

En Inglés: To be angry with someone

Context:

This one is pretty easy to use. The structure and translation is very similar to the English phrase "to be angry with someone." Hopefully you'll only use this when describing someone else's anger—not your own.

Dialogue:

Margarita: ¡Estoy enojado contigo, Pedro!

(I am angry with you Pedro!)

Pedro: ¿Con migo? ¿Por qué mi amigo?

(With me? Why my friend)

Margarita: Porque te olvidas que ayer fue mi cumpleaños.

(Because you forgot that yesterday was my birthday.)

Now Practice: Estar enojado con alguien

Repeat 3 times aloud, slowly

---

19) Can I ask you something?

En Español: ¿Puedo hacerte una pregunta?

En Inglés: Can I ask you a question?

Context:

This is more for use in familiar settings. You probably wouldn't say this to a stranger on the street. On the street, you might say, "Perdon." And then directly ask your question. This is more of a lead in to asking a more serious question of someone you are familiar with.

Dialogue:

Margarita: ¿Puedo hacerte una pregunta?

(Can I ask you a question?)

Pedro: ¡Por supuesto!

(Of course!)

Now Practice: ¿Puedo hacerte una pregunta?

Repeat 3 times aloud, slowly

---

20) Not very smart

En Español: Corto de luces

En Inglés: Not very smart/Not too bright

Context:

This directly translates to: "short of lights." We might say "not the sharpest tool in shed." Or "not the brightest bulb in the box." It describes someone that isn't very smart and it's more of a funny expression. If you're telling a story and use this expression, you'll probably make your friends laugh. But be careful, you don't want to say this around people you don't know or in formal company because you may offend someone.

Dialogue:

Margarita: No me gusta mi trabajo.

(I don't like my job)

Pedro: ¿Por qué no?

(Why not?)

Margarita: Porque mi jefe es corto de luces.

(Because my boss isn't very smart).

Now Practice: Corto de luces

Repeat 3 times aloud, slowly

21) I'll be right back

En Español: regreso en un momentito

En Inglés: I'll be right back

Context:

To use in a situation where you just need to step out for a moment or need to go get something quickly. It directly translates to: I'll return in a moment.

Dialogue:

Margarita: ¿Adonde vas Pedro?

(Where are you going, Pedro?)

Pedro: Voy al baño. Regreso en un momentito.

(I'm going to the bathroom. I'll be right back)

Margarita: ¡Rapido! Jajajaja

(Quickly! Hahaha)

Now Practice: Regreso en un Momentito

Repeat 3 times aloud, slowly

22) You've hit the nail on the head

En Español: Has dado en el clavo

En Inglés: You've hit the nail on the head

Context:

Just like the English colloquial expression this is a phrase you can use when someone gets it exactly right. When they explain something perfectly or make a point that you completely agree with.

Dialogue:

Margarita: Mi madre no está feliz conmigo.

(My mother is not happy with me)

Pedro: ¿Por qué? ¿Por qué

 nunca pasas tiempo con ella?

(Why? Is it because you never spend time with her?)

Margarita: Has dado en el clavo

(You've hit the nail on the head)

Now Practice: Has dado en el clavo

Repeat 3 times aloud, slowly

23) You're right

En Español: Tienes razón

En Inglés: You're right

Context:

This literally translates to: you have reason. This is a great way to agree with someone. If they say something you agree with you can just say "Tienes razón."

Dialogue:

Margarita: Es mejor si nos encontramos después de trabajo. Tendremos más tiempo.

(It's better if we meet after work. We will have more time)

Pedro: Si. Tienes Razón. Hasta entonces.

(Yes, you're right. See you then.)

Now Practice: Tienes razón

Repeat 3 times aloud, slowly

24) I'm not sure

En Español: No estoy seguro.

En Inglés: I'm not sure

Context:

This one is self-explanatory. For added emphasis, you can say "No estoy muy seguro," which means "I'm not really sure."

Dialogue:

Margarita: A qué hora empieza la película?

(What time does the movie start?)

Pedro: No estoy seguro. Dejame comprobar.

(I'm not sure. Let me check.)

Now Practice: No estoy seguro

Repeat 3 times aloud, slowly

25) What do you recommend?

En Español: ¿Qué me recomienda?

En Inglés: What do you recommend?

Context:

This can be used in all sorts of contexts: asking friends for recommendations about where to go and what to see and do in a new city, or else asking the waiter at the restaurant what dishes he recommends. Use it the same way you'd use the English phrase, "What do you recommend?"

Dialogue:

Margarita: Estoy en ese restaurante del que estabas hablando.

(I'm at that restaurant you were talking about.)

Pedro: ¿Oh enserio? ¿Qué vas a tomar?

(Oh really? What are you going to have?)

Margarita: No puedo decidir. ¿Qué me recomienda?

(I can't decide. What do you recommend?)

Now Practice: ¿Qué me recomienda?

Repeat 3 times aloud, slowly

26) Dude/Mate

En Español: Tío/Tía

En Inglés: Dude

Context:

Although the translation of Tío/Tía is uncle/aunt, in slang Spanish it means dude. If you're a young person or talking to a young person, it's great word to add to your vocabulary.

Dialogue:

Margarita: ¿Qué pasa tío?

(What's up dude?)

Pedro: Nada tía. ¿Cómo te ha ido?

(Nothing girl. How've you been?)

Now Practice: Tío…Tía…

Repeat 3 times aloud, slowly

---

27) I'm craving something

En Español: Tener el mono

En Inglés: I'm having a craving for…

Context:

This is a funny expression because it literally translates to: "to have the monkey." We're not sure where this phrase came from, but it's very popular especially with the hip, young crowd. The closest translation we can come up with is "to have a craving for…" or perhaps "I'm jonesing for…"

Dialogue:

Margarita: ¿Tienes hambre?

(Are you hungry?)

Pedro: Si. ¿Vamos al restaurante ahora?

(Yes. Are we going to the restaurant now?)

Margarita: Si! Tengo mono de papas fritas.

(Yes. I am craving french fries)

Now Practice: Tener el mono

Repeat 3 times aloud, slowly

---

28) Don't worry

En Español: No te preocupes

En Inglés: Don't worry

Context:

This translates seamlessly to English. Use this expression the same way you would use the English expression "Don't worry."

<u>**Dialogue:**</u>

Margarita: No me siento bien. Estoy muy enfermo.

(I don't feel well. I am very ill)

Pedro: ¿En serio? Hay algo que puedes hacer para ayudarte?

(Really? Is there anything I can do to help you?)

Margarita: No te preocupes. Voy a ir al doctor mañana.

(Don't worry. I am going to go to the doctor tomorrow).

Now Practice: No te preocupes

Repeat 3 times aloud, slowly

29) It's no big deal

En Español: No es para tanto

En Inglés: It's no big deal/It's not a big deal

Context:

The literal translation doesn't exactly make sense in English, but the meaning is roughly "It's not a big deal." This expression can be used as a gracious response in casual situations. Especially if you've been inconvenienced and someone is apologizing to you.

Dialogue:

Margarita: Lo siento, Pedro. Me olvide a pagarte por los boletos.

(I'm sorry Pedro. I forgot to pay you for the tickets.)

Pedro: No es para tanto. Puedes pagarme más tarde.

Now Practice: No es para tanto.

Repeat 3 times aloud, slowly

---

30) Cool!

En Español: ¡Qué guay!

En Inglés: How cool!

Context:

This expression is especially used by young people and is a good alternative to "Que Bueno," or any other affirmative expressions. Similar to English use of the word "cool" there are many different ways this phrase can be used.

Dialogue:

Margarita: Voy a Europa la próxima mes.

(I am going to Europe next month.)

Pedro: ¡Qué guay! Estoy tan celoso jajaja

(How cool! I'm so jealous hahaha)

Now Practice: ¡Qué guay!

Repeat 3 times aloud, slowly

---

31) No way!

En Español: ¡Venga ya!

En Inglés: No way/Come on!

Context:

This expression is especially popular in Spain and parts of Latin America. It's similar to the English phrase "come on" or "no way." If someone says something unbelievable or surprising you can say "Venga ya" or even just "venga."

Dialogue:

Margarita: ¿Fuiste al casino anoche?

(Did you go to the casino last night?)

Pedro: Si. Perdí mil dólares.

(Yes. I lost 1000 dollars)

Margarita: ¡Venga ya! ¿Qué paso?

(No way! What happened?)

Now Practice: ¡Venga ya!

Repeat 3 times aloud, slowly

---

32) To be very sure

En Español: Caerse de Madres
En Inglés: To be very sure (of something)/Fall head over heels

Context:

This expression is very common in Mexico, Spain, Puerto Rico and other parts of the world. The meaning changes slightly from region to region, but generally it means "to be very sure of something," or can also commonly mean "to be head over heels for someone," if you really, really like someone.

Dialogue:

Margarita: Pienso que Jorge me quiere.

(I think that Jorge loves me.)

Pedro: Si. El cae de madre para ti.

(Yes. He is head over heels for you)

Now Practice: Caerse de Madres

Repeat 3 times aloud, slowly

33) Always room for one more

En Español: Donde comen dos, comen tres

En Inglés: Always room for one more

Context:

This literally translates to: "when they eat two, they eat three." The closest idiomatic translation would be the English phrase "there's always room for one more." It's a nice welcoming phrase you may use especially when making new friends. This phrase is common in Puerto Rico.

Dialogue:

Margarita: ¿Cuándo vas al restaurant?

(When are you going to the restaurant?)

Pedro: Mis amigos y yo vamos A las doce y media.

(My Friends and I are going at 12:30)

Margarita: Bueno. ¿Puedo unirme a ustedes?

(Great. Can I join you?)

Pedtro: Por su puesto. Donde comen dos, comen tres.

(Of course. There's always room for one more.)

Now Practice: Donde comen dos, comen tres

Repeat 3 times aloud, slowly

---

34) Can I help you?

En Español: ¿Te ayudo?

En Inglés: Can I help you?

Context:

Although this translates directly to "I help you." It's popularly understood as "Can I help you?" It's shorter and easier than saying ¿Puedo ayudarte? Both phrases are correct but you may hear more people simply saying: ¿Te ayudo?

Dialogue:

Margarita: Tengo demasiado tarea esté noche...

(I have too much homework tonight...)

Pedro: ¿Te ayudo? Soy muy inteligente.

(Can I help you? I'm very smart)

Margarita: jajaja. No gracias. No lo creo.

(hahaha no thanks. I don't believe you.)

Now Practice: ¿Te ayudo?

Repeat 3 times aloud, slowly

---

35) Sweet dreams

En Español: Que sueñes con los ángeles

En Inglés: Sweet dreams (Sleep well)

Context:

The direct translation is "That you dream with the angels." This is a common greeting to say when you're going to bed or hanging up the phone with someone before they go to bed. Use it the same way you'd use the English expression: "Sweet dreams."

Dialogue:

Margarita: Necesito ir a cama. Estoy tan cansado.

(I need to go to bed. I'm so tired).

Pedro: Buenas noches Margarita. Que sueñes con los ángeles,

(Goodnight Margarita. Sweet dreams.)

Now Practice: Que sueñes con los ángeles

Repeat 3 times aloud, slowly

---

36) Are you done?

En Español: ¿Acabaste?

En Inglés: Are you done/Did you finished?

Context:

The verb most people learn to finish or end is terminar. But if you're asking if someone is finished with some task it's more correct to use: Acabaste.

Dialogue:

Margarita: ¿Acabaste la tarea?

(Did you finish your homework?)

Pedro: No. Ni siquiera lo he empezado.

(No. I haven't even started it.)

Margarita: ¿En Serio? ¡Date prisa tío!

(Seriously? Hurry up dude!)

Now Practice: ¿Acabaste?

Repeat 3 times aloud, slowly

---

37) Hurry up!

En Español: ¡Darse prisa!

En Inglés: Hurry Up

Context:

This literally translates to "give hurry." Since it's a reflexive verb, if you're giving it as a command you'd say "Date prisa" or if you're speaking formally to someone you don't know well or have a formal relationship, you'd say "Dale prisa." But since this is a casual command you wouldn't really use it in formal company. If you're saying someone has to hurry up. For example: you have to hurry up, then you'd use the form: Tienes que darte prisa changing the ending of tener and keeping the verb "dar" in the infinitve.

Dialogue:

Margarita: Todavía no estoy listo para el concierto. Necesito diez minutos más.

(I'm not ready for the concert yet. I need 10 more minutes.)

Pedro: Vale, pero date prisa.

(Okay but hurry up)

Now Practice: ¡Darse prisa!

Repeat 3 times aloud, slowly

38) In the blink of an eye

En Español: En un abrir y cerrar de ojos

En Inglés: in the blink of an eye

Context:

This literally translates to "in an open and close of the eyes." It is used to describe when something happens very quickly or when time seems to pass very quickly.

Dialogue:

Margarita: No puedo creer que ya termine con la universidad.

(I can't believe that I'm already finished with college.)

Pedro: No puedo creerlo tampoco

(I can't believe it either.)

Margarita: El tiempo pasó en un abrir y cerrar de ojos.

(The time passed in the blink of an eye.)

Now Practice: En un abrir y cerrar de ojos

Repeat 3 times aloud, slowly

---

39) To flip a coin

En Español: Jugársela a cara o cruz

En Inglés: To flip a coin

Context:

This literally translates to: "To play flip or flop." This phrase can be used literally if you actually want to flip a coin to determine something or if you're speaking figuratively about taking chances "the proverbial flip of a coin."

Dialogue:

Margarita: Juguemos futbol.

(Let's play soccer.)

Pedro: Vale. ¿Quién recibe la pelota primero?

(Ok. Who get's the ball first?)

Margarita: Podemos jugársela a cara o cruz.

(We can flip a coin.)

Now Practice: Jugársela a cara o cruz

Repeat 3 times aloud, slowly

---

40) Better late than never

En Español: Más vale tarde que nunca

En Inglés: Better late than never.

Context:

This basically has the same meaning and translation as the English equivalent. You could also say, "Mejor tarde que nunca," but saying, "Más vale tarde que nunca" sounds better and is more popularly used.

Dialogue:

Margarita: ¿Cuando llegas? Estoy esperando.

(When will you arrive? I'm waiting.)

Pedro: Todavía estoy a una hora de distancia.
(I'm still an hour away)

Margarita: Más vale tarde que nunca.

(Better late than never.)

Now Practice: Más vale tarde que nunca.

Repeat 3 times aloud, slowly

41) It goes without saying

En Español: Es cosa sabida

En Ingels: It goes without saying.

Context:

This directly translates to "It's a known thing." In english we say "It goes without saying." It usually is a response or a preface we use before saying something we think people automatically know or already agree with.

Dialogue:

Margarita: ¿Cómo fue la playa?

(How was the beach?)

Pedro: Solo más o menos. El clima estaba malo.

(It was only okay. The weather was bad.)

Margarita: Es cosa sabida que la playa es mas bonita cuando hace sol. Pero, ¿te divertiste de todos modos?

(It goes without saying that the beach is prettier when it is sunny, but did you have fun anyway?)

Now Practice: Es cosa sabida

Repeat 3 times aloud, slowly

---

42) Anyway

En Español: de todos modos

En Inglés: anyway

Context:

This directly translates to: "of all modes." Use it the same way you would use the English word "Anyway."

Dialogue:

Margarita: ¿Qué hora es?

(What time is it?)

Pedro: Las nueve y media

(9:30)

Margarita: La película ya ha comenzado. Podemos ir de todos modos si quieres.

(The movie has already started. We can go anyway if you want.)

Now Practice: de todos modos

Repeat 3 times aloud, slowly

---

43) At any cost

En Español: a como dé lugar

En Inglés: at any cost/at any price

Context:

This phrase doesn't have a good direct translation but generally it's an exclamation or phrase you can add to a sentence for extra emphasis if you want to show how important something is.

Dialogue:

Margarita: ¿Cómo están tus clases?

(How are your classes?)

Pedro: ¡Horrible! Mis notas son mediocres.

(Horrible! My grades are bad.)

Margarita: Quizás necesitas estudiar más. Necesitas terminar la universidad a como dé lugar.

(Maybe you need to study more. You need to finish college at any cost.)

Now Practice: a como dé lugar

Repeat 3 times aloud, slowly

---

44) In a nutshell

En Español: En pocas palabras

En Inglés: In a nutshell

Context:

This directly translates to "In a few words." Similar to the English expression "in a nutshell," this phrase is used if you're explaining something and are trying to sum something up or "make a long story short."

Dialogue:

Margarita: Tengo que romper con mi novio.

(I think I need to break up with my boyfriend.)

Pedro: ¿Por qué? ¿Qué Paso?

(Why? What happened?)

Margarita: En pocas palabras, creo que no tenemos futuro juntos.

(In a nutshell, I think we don't have a future together.)

Now Practice: En pocas palabras

45) To break up with

En Español: romper con

En Inglés: to break up with (someone)

Context:

This directly translates to "to break with." Hopefully you will not have to use this phrase too much but it's a good phrase to know if you're watching tv or if friends are talking to you about their lives or the lives of their friends.

Dialogue:

Margarita: ¿Has hablado con Catarina?

(Have you talked to Catarina?)

Pedro: No. Qué tal con ella

(No. What's up with her?)

Margarita: Ella va a romper con Jacobo esta noche.

(She is planning to break up with Jacobo tonight.)

Now Practice: romper con

Repeat 3 times aloud, slowly

46) To be crazy

En Español: Le falta un tornillo

En Inglés: a couple of screws loose

Context:

This directly translates to: "missing a screw." Much like the English phrase "a couple of screws loose," this is a phrase we use to describe people we think are a little crazy or who don't seem to be all there.

Dialogue:

Pedro: Tuve una cita anoche.

(I had a date last night.)

Margarita: ¿Cómo fue?

(How did it go?)

Pedro: La chica es bonita, pero le falta un tornillo.

(The girl was pretty but she was crazy).

Now Practice: Le falta un tornillo

Repeat 3 times aloud, slowly

47) To mess things up

En Español: Meter la pata

En Inglés: to screw up/mess up

Context:

This literally means: "put the paw in." It's a good way of saying "screw up" or "mess up." Meter is an infinitive verb so you can change the ending depending on what you are trying to say.

Dialogue:

Margarita: Metiste la pata.

(I screwed up)

Pedro: Qué Paso?

(What happened?)

Margarita: Me quede dormido esta mañana, y llegue a trabajo muy tarde.

(I overslept this morning and I arrived at work very late.)

Now Practice: Meter la pata

Repeat 3 times aloud, slowly

48) To be direct/straightforward

En Español: Poner el dedo en la llaga

En Inglés: to be direct about something

Context:

This directly translates to "put the finger in the wound." It basically means to get straight to the root or cause of the problem. It can also be like "putting salt in the wound," if it's a problem people don't want you to know about.

Dialogue:

Margarita: No hables con Mercedes sobre el trabajo ahora.

(Don't talk to Mercedes about work right now.)

Pedro: ¿Por qué no?

(Why not?)

Margarita: Porque ella ella perdió su trabajo. No quieres poner el dedo en la llaga.

(Because she lost her job. You don't want to put salt in the wound.)

Now Practice: Poner el dedo en la llaga

Repeat 3 times aloud, slowly

---

49) Open a can of worms

En Español: Abrir la caja de los truenos

En Inglés: Open a can of worms/Open Pandora's box

Context:

This directly means: open the box of thunder. You can use it like the English phrase "open a can of worms." This can describe when someone brings up a topic that makes everyone upset or argumentative.

Dialogue:

Margarita: Hablamos sobre tu ex novia.

(Let's talk about your ex girlfriend.)

Pedro: No creo que sea una buena idea. No quiero abrir la caja de truenos.

(I don't think that's a good idea. I don't want to open a can of worms)

Now Practice: Abrir la caja de los truenos

Repeat 3 times aloud, slowly

---

50) Beggars can't be choosers

En Español: al hambre no hay pan duro

En Inglés: beggars can't be choosers

Context:

This directly translates to: "for the hungry, there is no stale bread." This basically means if you don't have much, you can't expect much. You may not have cause to use this phrase much, but you may very well hear other people use it when describing situations or telling stories.

Dialogue:

Margarita: No me gusta esta camiseta con descuento. Me gusta esta costosa camisa.

(I do not like this discounted shirt. I like this expensive shirt.)

Pedro: Entonces, ¿cual es el problema?

(So what's the problem?)

Margarita: No tengo mucho dinero para comprar camisas caras.

(I don't have much money to buy expensive shirts.)

Pedro: Al hambre no hay pan duro.

(Beggars cant be choosers.)

Now Practice: Al hambre no hay pan duro.

Repeat 3 times aloud, slowly

---

51) Beat around the bush

En Español: Andarse por las ramas/Andar con rodeos

En Inglés: Talk evasively/Beat around the Bush

Context:

This directly translates to, "to walk in the branches." It's used when someone is evading the root cause of the matter or talking in circles. Use it the same way you'd use the English expression, "to beat around the bush." Another common way to say this expression is "andar con rodeos." They both mean the same thing but might vary in popularity from region to region.

Dialogue:

Margarita: ¿Peleas tú y tu novia?

(Are you and your girlfriend fighting?)

Pedro: De qué estás hablando

(What are you talking about)

Margarita: No hay necesidad a andar con rodeos. Yo vi que estabas discutiendo con ella antes.

(There's no need to beat around the Bush. I saw that you were arguing with her earlier.)

Now Practice: Andarse por las ramas

Andar con rodeos

Repeat 3 times aloud, slowly

---

52) To flirt with/Hit on (someone)

En Español: le tira los tejos

En Inglés: flirting with someone

Context:

This directly translates to: "to throw the yew trees." But in popular speech it means "to hit on someone" to "flirt with someone" to "make eyes at someone." Etc.

Dialogue:

Margarita: ¿Viste a Sabrina en la fiesta anoche?

(Did you see Sabrina at the party last night?)

Pedro: Si. Ella me estaba tirando los tejos toda la noche.

(Yes. She was hitting on me all night.)

Now Practice: tira los tejos

Repeat 3 times aloud, slowly

53) To be broke

En Español: Estar sin blanca

En Inglés: to be broke/to be hard up

Context:

This literally translates to "to be without white." This is a very common phrase in many Spanish speaking regions that means "to be broke" or to have no money.

Dialogue:

Margarita: ¿Quieres ir al concierto conmigo?

(Do you want to go to the concert with me?)

Pedro: No puedo. Estoy sin blanca.

(I can't. I'm broke).

Now Practice: Estar sin blanca

Repeat 3 times aloud, slowly

54) Good Luck!

En Español: ¡Buena suerte!

En Inglés: Good luck!

Context:

This is used exactly the same as the English phrase. The translation is directly "good luck."

Dialogue:

Margarita: Estoy muy nervioso sobre el examen de biología el viernes.

(I am very nervous about the biology exam on Friday)

Pedro: ¿Has estudiado?

(Have you studied?)

Margarita: Si. Mucho.

(Yes. A lot)

Pedro: Entonces, No pasa nada. ¡Buena suerte!

(Then don't worry about it. Good luck!)

Now Practice: ¡Buena suerte!

Repeat 3 times aloud, slowly

55) Have a snack

En Español: Matar el gusanillo

En Inglés: have a snack/kill a sweet tooth

Context:

This directly translates to: "Kill the worm." We don't have an exact translation in English but you can think of it like "killing hunger" having a snack to hold you over.

Dialogue:

Margarita: ¿Cuando vamos a la cena?

(When are we going to dinner?)

Pedro: No por tres horas más.

(Not for 3 more hours)

Margarita: Entonces voy a comer algo ahora. Necesito matar el gusanillo.

(Then I'm going to eat something now. I need something to hold me over.)

Now Practice: Matar el gusanillo

Repeat 3 times aloud, slowly

56) Enjoy your meal

En Español: Buen provecho

En Inglés: Have a nice meal/Enjoy your meal

Context:

This translates roughly to "Good advantage," or "Good profit," but it's very similar to the French: Bon Appetite. While you may not have a need to use this phrase, you will probably hear it very often when dining out in Spanish speaking countries so it's good to know what they're saying.

Dialogue:

Margarita: ¿Qué haces?

(What are you doing?)

Pedro: Cenando en restaurant con mi hermano.

(Eating dinner in a restaurant with my brother)

Margarita: Ahh, entonces llámame más tarde. ¡Buen provecho!

(Oh then call me later. Enjoy your meal!)

Now Practice: Buen provecho

Repeat 3 times aloud, slowly

57) What do you think?

En Español: ¿Qué te parece?

En Inglés: What do you think?/What does it seem?

Context:

This directly translates to: what does it seem to you? But it generally means, "What do you think?" You can also say, "¿Qué piensas?" both are ways of saying, "what do you think?"

Dialogue:

Margarita: ¿Leíste el email de Profesor Ramírez?

(Did you read the email from Professor Ramirez?)

Pedro: Si. Lo acabo de leer.

(Yes. I just read it.)

Margarita: ¿Y? ¿Qué te parece?

(And? What do you think?)

Now Practice: ¿Qué te parece?

Repeat 3 times aloud, slowly

---

58) Are you kidding?

En Español: ¿Estás de coña?

En Inglés: Are you kidding?/Are you kidding me?

Context:

This doesn't really have a direct translation. The word coña doesn't exactly mean anything outside of the context of "¿estás de coña?" This is a very casual phrase so only use it with friends.

Dialogue:

Margarita: Enrique y yo nos separamos.

(Enrique and I broke up.)

Pedro: ¿estás de coña?

(Are you kidding me?)

Now Practice: ¿Estás de coña?

Repeat 3 times aloud, slowly

---

59) Better than nothing

En Español: Peor es nada

En Inglés: Better than nothing

Context:

This directly translates to "worse is nothing." But can be likened to the English phrase: "Better than nothing."

Dialogue:

Margarita: ¿Cuánto tiempo tenemos juntos esta noche?

(How much time do we have together tonight?)

Pedro: Desafortunadamente, solo una hora. Necesito ayudar a mi mama con algo después.

(Unfortunately, only one hour. I need to help my mom with something after.)

Margarita: Ahh Está bien. Peor es nada.

(Oh it's okay. Better than nothing.)

Now Practice: Peor es nada

Repeat 3 times aloud, slowly

---

60) No if's and's or but's

En Español: no hay pero que valga

En Inglés: No if's and's or but's

Context:

This literally translates to "there is not but what is worth." It doesn't exactly make sense, but the closest English phrase would be, "No if's and's or but's." This is something you can say when you want something to sound very definitive—no argument.

Dialogue:

Pedro: ¿Estás seguro de que puedes venir conmigo a la casa de mi madre hoy?

(Are you sure you can come with me to my mom's house today?)

Margarita: Si. Claro que si. estaré allí no hay pero que valga.

(Yes of course. I will be there no if's and's or but's.)

Now Practice: no hay pero que valga

61) Of course

En Español: Claro que si

En Inglés: Of course

Context:

This translates to "clearly yes," but means "of course." You can also say "por su puesto" for of course. "Claro que si," is another way to say it.

Dialogue:

Margarita: ¿Te gusta chocolate?

(Do you like chocolate?)

Pedro: ¡Claro que sí! ¿Quien no?

(Of course! Who doesn't.)

Now Practice: Claro que si

62) Perfect match

En Español: tal para cual

En Inglés: birds of a feather/two of a kind

Context:

This means "perfect match," or "two peas in a pod," or "two of a kind." It literally translates to "such for which" but doesn't really make sense in English. Just use it the way you would use the English expression: "a perfect match."

Dialogue:

Margarita: ¿Qué piensas?

(what are you thinking?)

Pedro: …que yo quiero pizza.

(that I want pizza)

Margarita: ¡Eso es lo que estaba pensando también! Somos tal para cual.

(That's what I was thinking too!

Now Practice: tal para cual

Repeat 3 times aloud, slowly

63) Actions speak louder than words

En Español: Las palabras se las lleva el viento

En Inglés: actions speak louder than words

Context:

This directly translates to "words are gone in the wind," it basically means: "talk is cheap." Or "Actions speak louder than words."

Dialogue:

Margarita: ¿Por qué estas triste?

(Why are you sad?)

Pedro: Porque mi novia no cree que la amo, aunque le digo todo el tiempo.

(Because my girlfriend doesn't believe that I love her even though I tell her all the time.)

Margarita: Las palabras se las lleva el viento. Si la amas, muéstrale.

(Actions speak louder than words. If you love her, show her.)

Now Practice: Las palabras se las lleva el viento

Repeat 3 times aloud, slowly

64) Take care

En Español: ¡Cuídate!

En Inglés: Take care!

Context:

This is an appropriate thing to say when you're hanging up the phone or leaving someone in person. It roughly translates to the English phrase, "take care."

Dialogue:

Margarita: Tengo que irme ahora.

(I have to go now)

Pedro: ¿Tan temprano? ¿Por qué?

(So early? Why?)

Margarita: Tengo que acostarme. Necesito que levantarme temprano mañana.

(I have to go to bed. I need to get up early tomorrow.)

Pedro: Vale. ¡Cuidate! Buenos Noches.

(Ok. Take care. Good night.)

Now Practice: Cuidate

Repeat 3 times aloud, slowly

---

65) Behind (someone's) back

En Español: a las espaldas

En Inglés: behind your back

Context:

This directly translates to: "to the backs." It generally can describe when someone gossips secretly about someone else.

Dialogue:

Pedro: ¿Qué paso con Catrina anoche?

(What happened with Catrina last night?)

Margarita: Debes preguntarle a ti misma. Ella es mi amigo y no quiero hablar a las espaldas de ella.

(You should ask her yourself. She is my friend and I don't want to talk behind her back.)

Now Practice: a las espaldas

Repeat 3 times aloud, slowly

---

66) More of the same

En Español: ¿Qué le hace una mancha más al tigre?

En Inglés: More of the same/another nail in the coffin

Context:

This literally translates to "what's one more stripe to the tiger?" Generally this could mean "more of the same." Or sometimes it has a negative connotation like "one more nail in the coffin." But it is used to describe a situation where more of something you already have a lot of won't make much difference.

Dialogue:

Margarita: Mi jefe es tan molesto.

(My boss is so annoying)

Pedro: ¿Por qué dices eso?

(Why do you say that?)

Margarita: Siempre tenemos san muchos problemas a trabajo. ¿Qué le hace una mancha más al tigre?

(We always have so many problems at work. More of the same.)

Now Practice: ¿Qué le hace una mancha más al tigre?

Repeat 3 times aloud, slowly

---

67) So annoying

En Español: tan molesto

En Inglés: so annoying/bothersome

Context:

Hopefully you won't have to use this phrase too much, but it's very common among young people so you will almost certainly hear it when your friends are speaking.

Dialogue:

Margarita: Marco nunca me responde. Es tan molesto.

(Marco never responds to me. It's so annoying.)

Pedro: Quizás debes llamarle en lugar de le escribiendo.

(Maybe you should call him instead of texting him.)

Now Practice: tan molesto

Repeat 3 times aloud, slowly

68) It's a small world

En Español: El mundo es un pañuelo

En Inglés: it's a small world

Context:

This directly translates to: "the world is a handkerchief/scarf." While we're not sure where this phrase came from, it's very popularly used the way English speakers use the phrase "it's a small world," or "what a small world."

Dialogue:

Margarita: Mi hermana esta viajando en Sur America y conoció a alguien que te conoce.

(My sister is traveling in South America and she met someone who knows you.)

Pedro: ¿En serio? ¿Quién es? El mundo es un pañuelo.

(Really? Who is it? What a small world.)

Now Practice: El mundo es un pañuelo

Repeat 3 times aloud, slowly

69) It's better to be alone than in bad company

En Español: Más vale estar sólo que mal acompañado

En Inglés: It's better to be alone than with bad people

Context:

This directly translates to "It's better to be alone than badly accompanied." Although we don't really have an equivalent expression in English, this is a fairly common expression in Spanish Speaking countries.

Dialogue:

Margarita: No sé si debo salir esta noche con Marisol. No me gusta ella. ella es una mala amiga.

(I don't know if I should go out with Marisol tonight. I don't like her. She is a bad friend.)

Pedro: Entonces no vayas. Más vale estar sólo que mal acompañado.

(Then don't go. It's better to be alone than with bad company.)

Now Practice: Más vale estar sólo que mal acompañado

Repeat 3 times aloud, slowly

---

70) Best wishes for...

En Español: Los mejores deseos para...

En Inglés: best wishes to/for

Context:

This is an appropriate phrase if you're congratulating someone or if you're leaving an event or finishing a letter.

Dialogue:

Margarita: Vas a ir a la boda de Felipe y Consuela hoy?

(Are you going to Felipe and Consuela's wedding today?)

Pedro: Si. Acabo llegue.

(Yes I just arrived)

Margarita: Ahh. Ojalá pudiera estar allí. Diles que dije, "Los mejores deseos para la feliz día!"

(Ahh. I wish I could be there. Tell them I said, "¡Best wishes for the happy day!")

Now Practice: Los mejores deseos para…

Repeat 3 times aloud, slowly

---

71) Keep it on the dl/Mum's the word

En Español: En boca cerrada no entran moscas

En Inglés: keep quiet and mind your own business

Context:

This directly translates to: "flies can't enter a closed mouth." It's a popular phrase in Spain and other Spanish speaking countries when you want someone to mind their own business or keep something a secret.

Dialogue:

Margarita: ¿Qué dijo Jorge sobre mí?

(What did Jorge say about me?)

Pedro: No puedo decirte. Es un secreto.

(I can't tell you. It's a secret.)

Margarita: Dime. No le diré a nadie.

(Tell me. I won't tell anyone.)

Pedro: No puedo. En boca cerrada no entran moscas.

(I can't. I'm keeping i ton the dl.)

Now Practice: En boca cerrada no entran moscas

Repeat 3 times aloud, slowly

---

72) Sorry to interrupt

En Español: Siento interrumpir.

En Inglés: Excuse me/sorry to interrupt

Context:

This is a polite and more formal phrase you can use in public if you need to politely interrupt someone to ask a question. Of if you're at a restaurant, it's another way to get the attention of the staff although usually people will say "perdon" or excuse me.

Dialogue:

Margarita: Siento interrumpir, pero necesito saber si puedes venir a la fiesta esta noche.

(Sorry to interrupt, but I need to know if you can come to the party tonight.)

Pedro: No se todavía. Te lo haré saber.

(I don't know yet. I will let you know.)

Now Practice: Siento interrumpir.

Repeat 3 times aloud, slowly

73) I will let you know

En Español: Te lo haré saber.

En Inglés: I'll let you know

Context:

This is a helpful phrase to know and something you will hear a lot as well as use a lot in every day speech.

Dialogue:

Margarita: ¿Todavía vamos al cine esta noche?

(Are we still going to the movies tonight?)

Pedro: Si. ¿A qué hora?

(Yes. What time?)

Margarita: Depende de a qué hora termino el trabajo. Te lo haré saber.

(It depends on when I finish work. I will let you know.)

Now Practice: Te lo haré saber

Repeat 3 times aloud, slowly

74) Long time no see

En Español: ¡Tanto tiempo sin verte!

En Inglés: Long time no see

Context:

This literally translates to, "So long without seeing you." Use this phrase when greeting someone especially if you haven't seen/talked to them in a while.

Dialogue:

Margarita: ¡Oye! He vuelto de mis vacaciones.

(Hey! I'm back from vacation.)

Pedro: ¿Qué tal chica? ¡Tanto tiempo sin verte! ¿Disfrutaste tu vacaciones?

(What's up girl? Long time no see. Did you enjoy your vacation?)

Now Practice: ¡Tanto tiempo sin verte!

Repeat 3 times aloud, slowly

---

75) Welcome back

En Español: bienvenido de vuelto

En Inglés: welcome back!

Context:

This phrase is self-explanatory. You can use this with friends, colleagues or in any appropriate situation.

Dialogue:

Margarita: Finalmente me voy del hospital.

(Finally, I am leaving the hospital.)

Pedro: ¡Ahh bueno! ¡Bienvenido de vuelto! ¿Cómo te sientes?

(Oh great! Welcome back! How are you feeling?

Margarita: Mucho mejor. La medicina me ayuda mucho.

(Much better. The medicine is helping a lot.)

Now Practice: bienvenido de vuelto

Repeat 3 times aloud, slowly

76) Come again?

En Español: ¿De nuevo?

En Inglés: Come again/Pardon?

Context:

You may find this phrase to be very helpful especially when you're dealing with different accents and dialects of Spanish. If someone says something and you didn't quite catch it, you can say: "De Nuevo?" this roughly translates to: "Can you repeat that?" You can add por favor to make it sound more polite if you're in formal company. "De nuevo por favor?

Dialogue:

Margarita: Voy a llegar en unos minutos

(I will arrive in a few minutes)

Pedro: ¿De nuevo? La recepción de mi celular es mala. No te oí.

(Again? My cell reception is bad. I didn't hear you.)

Now Practice: ¿De nuevo?

Repeat 3 times aloud, slowly

77) What's done is done

En Español: A lo hecho, pecho

En Inglés: What's done is done

Context:

This literally translates to: "What's done, chest." Roughly this means "Chest out to deal with what's been done." It's an attitude that you can't change the past, so "what's done is done."

Dialogue:

Margarita: Creo que mi novio y yo Hemos roto para siempre esta vez.

(I think my boyfriend and I have broken up for good this time.)

Pedro: Que lastima. ¿Has intentado hablar con él?

(What a shame. Have you tried to talk to him?)

Margarita: Si, pero es inútil. A lo hecho, pecho

(Yes, but it's no use. What's done is done.)

Now Practice: A lo hecho, pecho

Repeat 3 times aloud, slowly

---

78) It's no use

En Español: es inútil

En Inglés: it's useless/no use

Context:

This directly translates to: "It's useless." But you can also say "No tiene sentido," which roughly translates to "it has no sense."

Dialogue:

Margarita: No puedo verte esta noche. Mi jefe me está haciendo trabajar hasta tarde.

(I can't see you tonight. My boss is making me work late.)

Pedro: Eso no es bueno. ¿Puedes hablar con él?

(That's no good. Can you talk to him?)

Margarita: Lo probé, pero es inútil.

(I tried, but it's no use.)

Now Practice: es inútil

Repeat 3 times aloud, slowly

---

79) For good

En Español: para siempre

En Inglés: For good/forever

Context:

This literally translates to "for forever." Although "forever" sounds more extreme than saying, "for good." Essentially, it means the same thing in conversation.

Dialogue:

Margarita: Decidí renunciar la carne para siempre.

(I decided to give up meat forever.)

Pedro: ¿En serio? Entonces eres vegetariano ahora.

(Really? Then you are a vegetarian now.)

Now Practice: para siempre

Repeat 3 times aloud, slowly

---

80) In spite of...

En Español: A pesar de que ...

En Inglés: In spite of/Although

Context:

This directly translates to "In spite of" or "despite." You can you it the same way you use the English phrase.

Dialogue:

Margarita: ¿Cómo va tu trabajo nuevo?

(How is your new job?)

Pedro: Me gusta en realidad. A pesar de que es un viaje largo a la oficina, todavía me gusta la compañía.

(I like it, actually. In spite of the long drive to the office, I still like the company.)

Now Practice: a pesar de que

Repeat 3 times aloud, slowly

81) In all detail

En Español: con pelos y señales

En Inglés: blow by blow/every detail

Context:

This literally translates to: "with hairs and signs." The closest equivalent expression in english would be: blow by blow or play by play. Basically you can use this expression when you want someone to spare no details.

Dialogue:

Margarita: ¿Qué hiciste anoche?

(What did you do last night?)

Pedro: Tuve una cita a ciegas.

(I had a blind date.)

Margarita: Que interesante. Dime todo con pelos y señales.

(Interesting! Tell me everything with every detail.)

Now Practice: con pelos y señales

Repeat 3 times aloud, slowly

---

82) to think you're center of the universe

En Español: creer a ser el ombligo del mundo
En Inglés: all about you/think the world revolves around you

Context:

This literally translates to: "to believe someone is the belly button of the world." Use this phrase like the phrase "to think the world revolves around (someone)."

Dialogue:

Margarita: Una vez más, mi jefe canceló nuestra reunión sin notificación.

(Once again, my boss canceled our meeting without notice.)

Pedro: Qué grosero.

(How rude.)

Margarita: Él no tiene respeto por mi tiempo. El cree que es el ombligo del mundo.

(He has no respect for my time. He thinks the world revolves around him)

Now Practice: creer a ser el ombligo del mundo

Repeat 3 times aloud, slowly

83) As soon as possible

En Español: cuanto antes

En Inglés: ASAP

Context:

This doesn't have a direct translation. Possibly "sooner," "how much before," but Spanish speakers use this phrase as English speakers use "as soon as possible."

Dialogue:

Margarita: Estoy esperando para ti en el restaurante.

(I am waiting for you at the restaurant.)

Pedro: Vale. Estaré allí cuanto antes.

(Ok. I'll be there as soon as possible.)

Now Practice: cuanto antes

Repeat 3 times aloud, slowly

84) On all fours

En Español: a gatas

En Inglés: on all fours/on hands and knees

Context:

This translates to "like cats." This makes sense when you think about it because cats walk on all fours.

Dialogue:

Margarita: ¿Cual Animal camina a gatas y tiene trompa?

(Which animal walks on all fours and has a trunk?)

Pedro: ¿un elefante?

(An elephant?)

Margarita: ¡Si! ¡Buen trabajo!

(Yes! Good work!)

Now Practice: a gatas

Repeat 3 times aloud, slowly

---

85) Beside the point

En Español: No viene al caso

En Inglés: not the point/beside the point

Context:

This directly translates to "does not come to the case," but you can use this any time you would use the English phrase, "beside the point."

Dialogue:

Margarita: ¿Sigues enojado conmigo?

(Are you still mad at me?)

Pedro: Un poco.

(A Little)

Margarita: Ya te dije que lo sentía

(I already told you I was sorry.)

Pedro: Eso no viene al caso. Necesitas pedir disculpas a mi novia.

(That's beside the point. You need to apologize to my girlfriend.)

Now Practice: No viene al caso

Repeat 3 times aloud, slowly

86) Give up

En Español: Darse por vencido

En Inglés: give up/throw in the towel

Context:

This roughly translates to "to give up" or "to give as defeated." As a reflexive verb you'll have to change the endings accordingly.

Dialogue:

Margarita: Estoy entrenando para un maratón, pero es demasiado difícil.

(I am training for a marathon, but it's too hard.)

Pedro: ¿Y ahora qué? ¿Quieres darse por vencido?

(And now what? Do you want to give up?)

Margarita: ¡Nunca!

(Never!)

Now Practice: Darse por vencido

Repeat 3 times aloud, slowly

---

87) Calm down

En Español: Calma, no hay prisa!

En Inglés: Calm down/what's the rush

Context:

This directly translates to "Calm down, there is no hurry," and can be likened to the English idiom, "hold your horses."

Dialogue:

Pedro: ¿A qué hora llegues?

(What time will you arrive?)
Margarita: A las seis y media.

(At 6:30)

Pedro: ¿En serio? Ughh tanto tiempo para esperar…

(Seriously? Ughh so long to wait…)

Margarita: ¡Calma, no hay prisa!

(Calm down, what's the rush?)

Now Practice: ¡Calma, no hay prisa!

Repeat 3 times aloud, slowly

---

88) For the heck of it

En Español: Por puro gusto

En Inglés: for no reason/for the heck of it

Context:

This translates to: "for pure pleasure." You can use this the way English speakers use the phrase: "just for the heck of it." Or "for the hell of it."

Dialogue:

Margarita: ¿Por qué tu hermano compró un auto nuevo?

(Why did your brother buy a new car?)

Pedro: Solo por puro gusto. Él le gustan autos y tiene dinero.

(Just for the heck of it. He likes cars and has money.)

Margarita: ¡Ah! ¡Debe ser bueno!

Now Practice: por puro gusto

Repeat 3 times aloud, slowly

---

89) To be on the fence

En Español: Nadar entre dos aguas

En Inglés: to be on the fence/undecided

Context:

This literally translates to: "to swim between two waters." The closest equivalent English expression would be, "to be on the fence." This can be used when you're torn between two options or you're undecided about something.

Dialogue:

Margarita: ¿Todavía quieres ir al parque? El clima es malo ahora.

(Do you still want to go to the park? The weather is bad now.)

Pedro: Estoy nadando entre dos aguas. Depende de ti.

(I'm on the fence. It's up to you.)

Now Practice: Nadar entre dos aguas

Repeat 3 times aloud, slowly

---

90) It's up to you

En Español: Depende de ti

En Inglés: It's up to you

Context:

This directly translates to: "it depends on you." For a more formal version, you can say: "Depende de usted."

Dialogue:

Margarita: ¿Cual tipo de comida quieres comer?

(What type of food do you want to eat?)

Pedro: No me importa. Depende de ti.

(I don't care. It depends on you.)

Now Practice: Depende de ti

Repeat 3 times aloud, slowly

---

91) I don't care

En Español: no me importa

En Inglés: I don't mind/I don't care

Context:

This can be used as "I don't care," if you want to express that you have no preference. You can use it as "I don't mind," also, if you want to express that something isn't bothering you.

Dialogue:

Margarita: ¿Quieres hablar esta noche o esperar hasta mañana?

(Do you want to talk tonight or wait until tomorrow.)

Pedro: No me importa. ¿Cuál es mejor para ti?

(I don't care. What's better for you?)

Now Practice: no me importa

Repeat 3 times aloud, slowly

92) Once in a while

En Español: De vez en cuando

En Inglés: Occasionally/Once in a while

Context:

This translates to something like: "Once in when," but use it the same way you'd use the English phrase, "once in a while," or "from time to time."

Dialogue:

Pedro: ¿Comes carne? Nunca te veo comiéndolo.

(Do you eat meat? I never see you eating it.)

Margarita: Si como carne de vez en cuando, pero solo pollo. Nunca como carne roja.

(Yes, I eat meat once in a while, but only chicken. I never eat red meat.)

Now Practice: De vez en cuando

93) Call a spade a spade

En Español: llamar al pan pan, y al vino vino

En Inglés: to call something like it is/to speak plainly

Context:

This directly translates to, "to call bread bread, and wine wine." The closest equivalent English phrase would be, "to call a spade a spade." To speak plainly about something or call something what it really is.

Dialogue:

Margarita: Cada vez hablo con María tengo que reír. Ella no es muy inteligente.

(Every time I talk to Maria I have to laugh. She is not very smart.)

Pedro: Llamamos al pan pan, y al vino vino. Ella es una idiota.

(Let's call a spade a spade. She is an idiot.)

Margarita: ¡Eres horrible! No eres tan inteligente tú mismo jajaja.

(You are horrible! You're not so smart yourself hahaha.)

Now Practice: llamar al pan pan, y al vino vino

Repeat 3 times aloud, slowly

94) At least

En Español: al menos

En Inglés: at least

Context:

This basically directly translates to "at least." Use it the same way you'd use the English equivalent.

Dialogue:

Margarita: Algunos días solo quiero dejar mi trabajo.

(Some days I just want to quit my job.)

Pedro: Al menos tienes un trabajo. Mi hermana todavía no ha encontrado un trabajo después de 3 meses de búsqueda.

(At least you have a job. My sister still has not found a job after 3 months of searching.)

Now Practice: al menos

Repeat 3 times aloud, slowly

---

95) To talk a lot

En Español: Hablar hasta por los codos

En Inglés: to talk your head off/talk a lot

Context:

This directly translates to, "to talk through the elbows," and basically can describe a situation where someone is talking a ridiculous amount.

Dialogue:

Margarita: Lo siento que estoy tarde.

(Sorry I'm late.)

Pedro: Sin preocupaciones.

(No worries.)

Margarita: Cada vez que tengo prisa, mi hermana quiere hablar hasta por los codos.

(Every time I'm in a hurry, my sister wants to talk her head off.)

Now Practice: Hablar hasta por los codos

Repeat 3 times aloud, slowly

---

96) To feel like (doing something)

En Español: tener ganas

En Inglés: to want to/to be in the mood to

Context:

This doesn't exactly translate, but it's an extremely popular way of saying you want to do something. This is especially popular in the Americas among young people. Use it the way you'd say, "I feel like (doing something)," or "I'm in the mood (to do something)."

Dialogue:

Margarita: ¿Planeas ir a la playa este fin de semana?

(Are you planning to go to the beach this weekend?)

Pedro: Si tengo ganas. Vamos a ver.

(If I feel like it. We'll see.)

Now Practice: tener ganas

Repeat 3 times aloud, slowly

---

97) To sleep on it

En Español: Consultar la almohada

En Inglés: to sleep on it

Context:

This directly translates to, "To consult (or check) the pillow." Similar to the English phrase of "sleeping on something," this is used when you want some time to think about something.

Dialogue:

Margarita: ¿Crees que deberíamos decirle a Luisa que Rogelio la está engañando?

(Do you think we should tell Luisa that Rogelio is cheating on her?)

Pedro: No se todavía. Consultamos la almohada y entonces decidimos.

(I don't know yet. Let's sleep on it and then decide.)

Now Practice: Consultar la almohada

Repeat 3 times aloud, slowly

98) To look the other way

En Español: Hacerse la vista gorda

En Inglés: to overlook/turn a blind eye

Context:

This literally translates to, "to make your vision (or eyes) fat." The closest equivalent English expression would be, "to turn a blind eye," or more simply, "to look the other way." This describes when someone purposely overlooks something (usually it has a negative connotation).

Dialogue:

Margarita: He llegado tarde al trabajo todos los días de esta semana.

(I've been late to work every day this week.)

Pedro: ¿Está enojado tu jefe?

(Is your boss angry?)

Margarita: No lo creo. Él ha estado haciendo la vista gorda.

(I don't think so. He has been turning a blind eye.)

Now Practice: Hacerse la vista gorda

Repeat 3 times aloud, slowly

---

99) Much ado about nothing

En Español: Mucho ruido y pocas nueces

En Inglés: a lot of fuss for no reason

Context:

This translates to, "a lot of noise and a few nuts." This could roughly be likened to the popular English phrase, "much ado about nothing." This describes a situation where everyone seems to be making a big deal out of nothing important.

Dialogue:

Margarita: ¿Por qué están tus vecinos de pie en la calle? Hay una gran multitud. ¿Qué paso?

(Why are your neighbors standing in the street. There's a big crowd. What happened?)

Pedro: Hubo un pequeño accidente de coche, pero nada serio. Mucho ruido y pocas nueces.

(There was a small car accident, but nothing serious. Much ado about nothing.)

Now Practice: Mucho ruido y pocas nueces

Repeat 3 times aloud, slowly

---

100) Rings a bell

En Español: Me suena

En Inglés: rings a bell

Context:

This can be used either positively or negatively. "Me suna," indicates something sounds familiar whereas, "no me suena," is how you'd say you cannot recall or that something doesn't ring a bell.

Dialogue:

Margarita: ¿Te acuerdas Katie Brown de escuela secundaria?

(Do you remember Katie Brown from high school?)

Pedro: Hmm…Ese nombre no me suena.

(Hmm… that name doesn't ring a bell.)

Now Practice: Me suena

Repeat 3 times aloud, slowly

---

101) Wake up

En Español: Ponte las pilas

En Inglés: snap out of it/wake up

Context:

This translates to: "Put in your batteries." While we don't have a directly equivalent phrase in English, it is used when you want someone to "Wake up" (not from sleep) if they are day dreaming or seem to be distracted or out of it. It can also be used to urge someone to "get cracking," or "get moving," on something.

Dialogue:

Margarita: ¿Qué estás planeando para el cumpleaños de tu novia?

(What are you planning for your girlfriend's birthday?)

Pedro: Uhh…no se todavía. No lo he pensado mucho.

(Uhh…I don't know yet. I haven't thought about it much.)

Margarita: ¡Ponte las pilas tío! ¡Su cumpleaños es el próximo sábado!

(Get on it dude! Her birthday is next Saturday!)

Now Practice: Ponte las pilas

Repeat 3 times aloud, slowly

Conclusion:

We hope you have enjoyed learning these phrases and expressions. Some of them are a lot of fun, some of them are practical and some are just strange. Nonetheless, in any context where you'll be having conversations in Spanish, you will have ample opportunities to put what you've learned to use both in speaking and listening.

The Spanish language is a poetic and colorful language that relies heavily on the usage of expressions, similes and idioms. By learning these 101 phrases you have greatly enriched your understanding of the Spanish language and have greatly improved your ability to communicate naturally with native speakers.

Many readers will find it helpful to read through this book several times and especially focus on the dialogues and repetition of the words and phrases to truly commit the contents of this book to memory. We wish you all the best on your self-educated language journey, and we hope we've been able to provide you with useful information that will speed you to greater heights of fluency.

Book 2:

Beyond Basics:

200 Essential Intermediate Spanish Phrases

for Fluent Conversation

Orbis Language Center

Introduction:

Congratulations on purchasing: *Beyond the Basics: 200 Essential Intermediate Spanish Phrases for Fluent Conversation.*

It's funny how in Spanish classes we can learn so many words and so much grammar, but then be at a total loss when it comes to actually having conversations in Spanish. The school system typically doesn't do a very good job of preparing students for speaking day-to-day Spanish. You might have been able to pass that vocabulary quiz, but that won't get you that far in Spanish speaking countries or if you want to be able to have fluent conversations in Spanish.

We start with a few of the basics like, "Hasta La proxima ves," or "De donde eres," just to get you warmed up and stay up on the foundational questions. We quickly progress to phrases you may not be as familiar with like, "Me lo estoy pasando bien," "which means "I'm having a good time," or phrases like, "Que hacer cola," which means, "to wait in line."

The goal of this book is to provide you with a generous supply of simple, incredibly useful Spanish phrases (most of which you probably haven't mastered yet), to help take your conversation skills to the next level.

This book also contains numerous idioms and colloquialisms which you will find both insightful and useful. Hispanic culture is incredibly colorful and each region has numerous local sayings and idioms, so I've only included really common ones that seem to be pretty universal across all Spanish speaking countries.

You will learn:

- The English and Spanish version of the idiom/phrase
- The explanation of how to use this idiom or phrase in common speech and when is an appropriate time to use it
- Examples of casual dialogue in both Spanish and English to show you the context of how this phrase is used
- You can practice repeating each phrase to help commit it to memory and work through the pronunciation

For best results, practice saying these phrases out loud. I've also found that writing the phrases down from memory on a scrap piece of paper whenever I have time also helps commit it all to memory. The more ways you can incorporate yourself into your learning, the more quickly you'll be able to master all these phrases. Listen carefully to the dialogues because we've tried to capture natural-sounding speech in which these phrases would be used so you have a very useful context in which to understand the phrase. As with all languages, there are often many ways to say what you want to say in Spanish. We've tried to include some different options here so you can start to get a more three-dimensional understanding of the language and how to say things different ways for different emphasis, or when you're in different types of company.

Of course, there are thousands of Spanish phrases you could learn, but out of the many options, we've selected the ones we find to be most overlooked and most beneficial and useful for natural conversation. As with all types of learning, it's always best to go little by little. 200 phrases is a great goal for mastery. Trying to master a book of 1000 or more phrases is simply too intimidating and difficult for most people to start out with.

We recommend going slowly through the book and going through it multiple times until you are comfortable with all of the phrases in terms of memory, pronunciation, and context. If you can go through the book with a partner, you can read the dialogues together for maximum learning potential.

So, let's get started with 200 Essential Intermediate Spanish Phrases for Fluent Conversation. Thank you for purchasing this book, and good luck with your studying, or we should say, "¡Buena suerte con sus estudios!"

---

1. Hasta La proxima ves—until next time!

(Use this phrase when walking out of a shop or restaurant or when taking leave of a friend.)

Dialogue:

Waiter at Restaurant: Gracias por venir, tener un gran día.

Thank you for coming, have a good day!

Margarita: Hasta La proxima ves, gracias.

Until next time. Thank you!

Now Practice: Hasta La proxima ves

Repeat Aloud 3 times slowly to practice

---

2. Saludos—Greetings!

(This is a more formal way of greeting someone)

Dialogue:

Margarita: Saludos, Pedro.

Greetings, Pedro.

Pedro: Hola Pedro, como esta?

Hello Pedro, how are you?

Now Practice: Saludos

Repeat Aloud 3 times slowly to practice

---

3. Me llamo—my name is

(This actually translates to, "Call me." So instead of saying, "My name is Debbie," You'd say, "Call me Debbie," or "Me llamo Debbie." People don't usually say, "Mi nombre es" which would be a more direct translation of "my name is.")

Dialogue:

Pedro: Come te llamas?

What is your name?

Margarita: Me llamo Margarita. Y tu?

My name is Margarita. What's yours?

Now Practice: Me llamo

Repeat Aloud 3 times slowly to practice

---

4. De donde eres?—Where are you from?

(You could also say, "de donde vienes?" which translates more closely to, "where do you come from?")

Dialogue:

Pedro: De donde eres?

Where are you from?

Margarita: Soy de España

I'm from Spain

Now Practice: De donde eres?

Repeat Aloud 3 times slowly to practice

---

5. Donde vives?—where do you live?
   (Obviously this is a different question from, "where are you from?" Don't get them mixed up.)

Dialogue:

Margarita: Donde vives ahora?

Where do you live now?

Pedro: Vivo cerca de Barcelona

I live near Barcelona.

Now Practice: Donde vives?

Repeat Aloud 3 times slowly to practice

---

6. Que hiciste hoy?—What did you do today?

Dialogue:

Margarita: Bievenido a casa! Que hiciste hoy?
Welcome home! What did you do today?
Pedro: Thanks! No hice mucho hoy.
Thank you! I didn't do very much today.

Now Practice Que hiciste hoy?

Repeat Aloud 3 times slowly to practice

---

7. ¿Qué tal tu día?—How was your day?

(NOTE: typically, que tal is used for "what's up?" so this is kind of like saying, "what's up with your day?" but is a casual way of asking someone how their day was.)

Dialogue:

Margarita: ¿Que tal tu día?

How was your day?

Pedro: Fue fantástico. Logré mucho.

It was great! I got a lot done.

Now Practice: ¿Que tal tu día?

Repeat Aloud 3 times slowly to practice

---

8. Que haces?—What are you doing?

(This is a way of asking someone what they're currently doing, and can also be used like the English term, "What's up?")

Dialogue:

Margarita: Que haces?

What are you doing?

Pedro: Estoy cenando ahora.

I'm eating dinner right now.

Now Practice: Que haces?

Repeat Aloud 3 times slowly to practice

---

9. Tengo mucho que hacer—I have a lot to do

(You could also say, "Tengo muchas cosas que hacer" which translates to, "There are many things to do." But you can use it when you're busy and you have a lot to do.)

Dialogue:

Margarita: Tienes tiempo para ir al cine esta noche?

Do you have time to go to the movies tonight?

Pedro: Probablemente no. Tengo mucho que hacer esta noche.

Probably not. I have a lot to do tonight.

Now Practice: Tengo mucho que hacer

Repeat Aloud 3 times slowly to practice

---

10. Que pasa?—What's happening?

(NOTE: you can use this to literally ask someone what is happening at that moment. If you wanted to simply ask someone what they're up to like the English phrase, "What's up," you could say, "que tal?")

Dialogue:

Margarita: Estaré en casa en unos minutos. Que pasa?

I will be home in a few minutes. What's happening?

Pedro: No estoy haciendo nada ahora

I'm not doing anything right now.

Now Practice: Que pasa?

Repeat Aloud 3 times slowly to practice

---

11. ¿Qué estás pensando?—What are you thinking about?

Dialogue:

Pedro: ¿Qué estás pensando, Margarita?

What are you thinking about, Margarita?

Margarita: Estoy pensando de mi estomago. Tengo mucho hambre.

I am thinking about my stomach. I am so hungry!

Now Practice: ¿Qué estás pensando?

Repeat Aloud 3 times slowly to practice

---

12. Esta bien—it's fine (it's okay)

(You can use this for all sorts of different responses. It can mean, "okay," "it's fine," "it's okay," "it's all good." Etc.)

Dialogue:

Margarita: Lo siento, llego tarde.

Sorry I'm late.

Pedro: Esta bien. No te preocupes.

It's okay. Don't worry about it.

Now Practice: Esta bien

Repeat Aloud 3 times slowly to practice

---

13. Es bueno verte!—It's so nice to see you

(Note. This is not what you say when meeting someone. You would say, "Encantado de conocerte," or just, "encantado," for someone you're just meeting. You'd say this with someone you already know that you haven't seen in a while.)

Dialogue:

Pedro: Es bueno verte, Margarita!

It's so nice to see you, Margarita!

Margarita: ¡Lo sé! Ha pasado mucho tiempo.

I know! It's been too long!

Now Practice: Es bueno verte

Repeat Aloud 3 times slowly to practice

---

14. ¿Como esta tu familia?—How is your family?

Dialogue:

Margarita: ¿Como esta tu familia?

How is your family?

Pedro: Estan bien. Mi hermana se caso la semana pasada.

They are well. My sister got married last week.

Now Practice: ¿Como esta tu familia?

Repeat Aloud 3 times slowly to practice

---

15. ¿Estás libre?—are you free?

(NOTE: this is how you'd ask someone if they're available to hang out)

Dialogue:
Pedro: Cuando podemos hablar?
When can we talk?
Margarita: ¿Estás libre esta noche?
Are you free tonight?

Now Practice: ¿estás libre?

Repeat Aloud 3 times slowly to practice

---

16. ¿Estas ocupado?—Are you busy

Dialogue:

Margarita: ¿Qué haces esta noche? ¿Estas ocupado?

What are you doing tonight? Are you busy?

Pedro: No, estoy libre. ¿Por qué? ¿Qué pasa?

No. I am free. Why? What's up?

Now Practice: ¿Estas ocupado?

Repeat Aloud 3 times slowly to practice

---

17. Es fácil—It's easy

Dialogue:

Margarita: ¿Puedes enseñarme a conducir manual?

Can you teach me how to drive manual?

Pedro: ¡Sí! ¡Es fácil!

Yes. It's easy!

Now Practice: Es fácil

Repeat Aloud 3 times slowly to practice

---

18. Es difícil—It's difficult

Dialogue:

Margarita: Estoy tratando de ahorrar dinero.

I am trying to save money.

Pedro: Yo también. ¡Es muy difícil!

I am too. It's so difficult!

Now Practice Es difícil

Repeat Aloud 3 times slowly to practice

---

19. le presentó —this is
    (Note: this is how you would introduce someone. You'd say, "Le presento Debbie," for "This is Debbie." This is a more informal way of speaking but will work for most occasions. You will hear it often).

    Dialogue:

    Margarita: Pedro, le presento a mi hermana, Sofia.

    Pedro, this is my sister, Sofia.

    Pedro: Encantado de conocerte, Sofia!

    It's nice to meet you, Sofia!

    Now Practice: le presentó

    Repeat Aloud 3 times slowly to practice

---

20. ¿Puede hablar más despacio?—could you speak more slowly?
    (Note: it's always nice to add a "por favor," to make this request more polite. Spanish-speakers can speak very fast sometimes, so you may find this phrase useful.)
    Dialogue:

    Margarita: ¿Puede hablar más despacio, por favor?

    Can you please speak more slowly?

    Pedro: ¡Por supuesto! Lo siento, siempre hablar demasiado rápidamente.

    Sure! Sorry, I always speak too fast.

    Now Practice: ¿Puede hablar más despacio?

    Repeat Aloud 3 times slowly to practice

---

21. ¿Puedes hablar un poco más fuerte por favor? --Can you speak a little more loudly please?
    (Much like the previous phrase, you may find this phrase useful as a non-native speaker. And of course, adding the "un poco" makes you sound politer.)

    Dialogue:

    Margarita: ¿Puedes hablar un poco más fuerte por favor?

    Sorry, can you speak a little louder please?

    Pedro: Estoy hablando en voz baja porque me duele la garganta.

    I'm speaking quietly because my throat hurts.

Now Practice: ¿Puedes hablar un poco más fuerte por favor?

Repeat Aloud 3 times slowly to practice

22. ¿Puedes repetirlo, por favor?—Could you repeat that please?
    (NOTE: this is more of a formal way of saying it. If you're in informal company, you can simply say, "De nuevo?" or more politely, "De nuevo por favor? Which means, "again?" or "again, please?")

    Dialogue:

    Margarita: ¿Puedes repetirlo, por favor? Estaba distraido

    Can you repeat that please? I was distracted.

    Pedro: Nunca me escuchas.

    You never listen to me

    Now Practice: ¿Puedes repetirlo, por favor?

    Repeat Aloud 3 times slowly to practice

23. Entiendo perfectamente—I understand perfectly

    (Note: You could also say, "entiendo claramente," for a little less emphasis.)

    Dialogue:

    Margarita: Escribí instrucciones para ti. ¿Entiendes?

    I wrote instructions for you. Do you understand?

    Pedro: Entiendo perfectamente.

    I understand perfectly.

    Now Practice: Entiendo perfectamente

    Repeat Aloud 3 times slowly to practice

24. Encantado de conocerte (Or you can just say, "encantado")—Nice to meet you
    (Note: This directly translates to, "pleasure of meeting," or if you just say, "Encantado," it just means "pleasure." Only use "encantado," in more relaxed informal settings. Please also note that if you are a woman, you'll use "encantada" regardless of the gender of the person you're speaking to. If you're a man, you'll use, "encantado" in the same way.)

Dialogue:

Margarita: Pedro, te presento a mi jefe, Lorenzo.

Pedro, meet my boss Lorenzo.

Pedro: Encantado de conocerte, Lorenzo

It's nice to meet you, Lorenzo.

Now Practice: Encantado de conocerte

Repeat Aloud 3 times slowly to practice

---

25. conocer a alguien —to meet someone
(Note: this is usually used when describing meeting someone for the first time and not often used to describe when two people "meet up" or "hang out."
Dialogue:

Margarita: Tienes que conocer a mi amiga, Blanca.

You have to meet my friend Blanca.

Pedro: Si me gustaria.

Yes, I would like to.

Now Practice: para conocer a alguien

Repeat Aloud 3 times slowly to practice

---

26. hacer el conocido de —to make the acquaintance of someone
(NOTE: this is a lot more formal than "conocer a alguien," but can be used in more formal situations when appropriate.)
Dialogue:

Margarita: Pedro, debes hacer el conocido de mi jefe, Julio.

Pedro, you should make the acquaintance of my boss, Julio.

Pedro: Si, presénteme por favor.

Yes, introduce me please.

Now Practice: hacer el conocido de

Repeat Aloud 3 times slowly to practice

---

27. todo va bien —everything's going well

Dialogue:

Margarita: ¿Como va todo de tu trabajo?

How's everything at work?

Pedro: Todo va bien gracias por preguntar.

Everything's going well, thanks for asking.

Now Practice: todo va bien

Repeat Aloud 3 times slowly to practice

---

28. Estoy bien, ¿Y tú?—I'm well, and you?
    (Note: if you're in a formal conversation, you can substitute "usted" for "tu?")

    Dialogue:

    Margarita: ¡Oye! ¿Como estas?

    Hey! How are you?

    Pedro: Estoy bien, ¿Y tú?

    I'm well, and you?

    Now Practice: Estoy bien, ¿Y tú?

    Repeat Aloud 3 times slowly to practice

    ---

29. ¿No puedo quejarme—I can't complain!

    Dialogue:

    Margarita: ¿Como va todo?

    How is everything?

    Pedro: ¡No puedo quejarme!

    I can't complain!

    Now Practice: ¡No puedo quejarme!

    Repeat Aloud 3 times slowly to practice

---

30. no está mal—Not bad

Dialogue:

Margarita: ¿Como va todo?

How is everything?

Pedro: No está mal, termine mucho trabajo.

Not bad, I got a lot of work done.

Now Practice: no está mal

Repeat Aloud 3 times slowly to practice

31. Muy bien, gracias—very well, thank you!

Dialogue:

Margarita: ¿Como esta tu madre?

How is your mother?

Pedro: Ella está muy bien, gracias.

She is very well, thank you.

Now Practice: Muy bien, gracias

Repeat Aloud 3 times slowly to practice

32. ¡Los mejores deseos!—Best wishes!

Dialogue:

Margarita: Hoy es mi cumpleaños.

Today is my birthday.

Pedro: ¿En serio? ¡Mis mejores deseos para ti, Margarita!

Oh really? My best wishes to you, Margarita!

Now Practice: ¡Los mejores deseos!

Repeat Aloud 3 times slowly to practice

33. ¡Buena suerte!—Good Luck!

Dialogue:

Margarita: Voy a mi entrevista en una hora.

I am going to a job interview in one hour.

Pedro: ¡Buena suerte!

Good luck!

Now Practice: ¡Buena suerte!

Repeat Aloud 3 times slowly to practice

34. Felicidades—Congratulations!

Dialogue:

Margarita: Mi hermana tuvo a su bebe. ¡Soy una tía ahora!

My sister had her baby. I am an aunt now!

Pedro: ¡Felicidades! ¿Como se llama, él bebe?

Congratulations! What is the baby's name?

Now Practice: ¡Felicidades!

Repeat Aloud 3 times slowly to practice

35. ¡Buen provecho!—Enjoy your meal
(NOTE: There's no direct English translation, but it's the same as the internationally popular French phrase, "Bon Apetit." But there are also many ways of saying this in Spanish. You may hear, "¡Buen apetito!," or simply "¡Provecho!")
Dialogue:

Margarita: Estoy cenando con mi familia ahora.

I'm eating dinner with my family right now.

Pedro: Ahh vale. ¡Buen provecho!

Oh okay. Enjoy your meal!

Now Practice: ¡Buen provecho!

Repeat Aloud 3 times slowly to practice

36. ¡Salud!—Cheers!

(Salud means, "To your health," some countries also say, "¡Dinero!" or other exclamations.)

Dialogue:

Margarita: ¡Bebamos para su promoción!

Let's drink to your promotion!

Pedro: ¡Salud!

Cheers!

Now Practice: ¡Salud!

Repeat Aloud 3 times slowly to practice

37. Mejorate pronto—Get well soon

Dialogue:

Margarita: No fui a trabajo hoy. Estoy enferma.

I didn't go to work today. I'm sick.

Pedro: Oh no. Espero que te mejores pronto

Oh no! I hope you get well soon!

Now Practice: Mejorate pronto

Repeat Aloud 3 times slowly to practice

38. ¡Feliz Navidad!—Merry Christmas
Dialogue:

Margarita: ¡Feliz Navidad, Pedro!

Merry Christmas, Pedro!

Pedro: ¡Igualmente!

The same to you!

Now Practice: ¡Feliz Navidad!

Repeat Aloud 3 times slowly to practice

39. ¡Feliz año nuevo!--Happy New Year!
Dialogue:

Margarita: ¡Feliz Navidad, Pedro!

Merry Christmas, Pedro!

Pedro: Feliz Navidad y Feliz año nuevo.

Merry Christmas and Happy New Year to you.

Now Practice: ¡Feliz año nuevo!

Repeat Aloud 3 times slowly to practice

---

40. ¡Felices pascuas!—Happy Easter!

Dialogue:

Margarita: ¡Felices pascuas!

Happy Easter!

Pedro: Gracias, Margarita

Thank you, Margarita

Now Practice: ¡Felices pascuas!

Repeat Aloud 3 times slowly to practice

---

41. ¿Qué es esto?—what is this?

Dialogue:

Margarita: ¿Qué es esto?

What is this?

Pedro: Es una carta de mi padre.

It's a letter from my father.

Now Practice: ¿Qué es esto?

Repeat Aloud 3 times slowly to practice

---

42. No sé —I don't know
Dialogue:

Margarita: ¿Qué hora es?

What time is it?

Pedro: No sé. No tengo reloj.

I don't know. I don't have a watch.

Now Practice: No sé

Repeat Aloud 3 times slowly to practice

---

43. Sí, lo sé —yes I know

    Dialogue:

    Margarita: Ya son las seis y media.

    It's already 6:30.

    Pedro: Sí, lo sé. Voy tarde.

    I know. I am late.

    Now Practice: Sí, lo sé

    Repeat Aloud 3 times slowly to practice

---

44. no lo hare —I won't do it

    Dialogue:

    Margarita: Deberías cantar karaoke esta noche.

    You should sing at karaoke tonight.

    Pedro: No lo hare.

    I won't do it

    Now Practice: no lo hare

    Repeat Aloud 3 times slowly to practice

---

45. No importa—It doesn't matter/ It's alright
    (NOTE: this directly translates to something like, "it's not important," if you wanted to say it doesn't matter to me, or "I don't care," you can say, "no me importa.")

    Dialogue:

    Margarita: Lo siento, me olvide de devolver la llamada

    I'm sorry I forgot to call you back.

Pedro: No importa, mi amiga.

It's alright my friend.

Now Practice: No importa

Repeat Aloud 3 times slowly to practice

---

46. Buenos dias — Good morning

(you can use this any time before lunch time.)

Dialogue:

Margarita: ¡Buenos días, Pedro!

Good morning, Pedro!

Pedro: Buenos días. ¿Como dormiste?

Good morning. How did you sleep?

Now Practice: Buenos dias

Repeat Aloud 3 times slowly to practice

47. Buenos tardes — Good afternoon
(you can use this anytime between lunch and dinner.)

Dialogue:

Margarita: Buenos tardes.

Good afternoon.

Pedro: Hi. ¿Como estuvo tu mañana?

Hi. How was your morning?

Now Practice: Buenos tardes

Repeat Aloud 3 times slowly to practice

48. Buena noche — Good evening
(you can use this from dinner time until about 9pm)

Dialogue:

Margarita: Buena noche, Pedro.

Good evening, Pedro.

Pedro: Buena noche. ¿Como estuvo tu día?

Good evening. How was your day?

Now Practice: Buena noche

Repeat Aloud 3 times slowly to practice

---

49. Buenas noches –Good Night
(this can be used late at night as a farewell, or you can say it to someone when they're headed to bed.)

Dialogue:

Margarita: Voy a acostarme ahora.

I am going to bed.

Pedro: Buenas noches. Duerma bien.

Good night. Sleep well.

Now Practice: Buenas noches

Repeat Aloud 3 times slowly to practice

---

50. ¡Que tenga un buen día!—Have a nice day!

Dialogue:

Margarita: Tengo que ir a trabajo ahora.

I have to go to work now.

Pedro: Vale. ¡Que tenga un buen día!

Alright. Have a nice day!

Now Practice: ¡Que tenga un buen día!

Repeat Aloud 3 times slowly to practice

---

51. ¡Igualmente!—same to you

Note: this roughly translates to, "equally." You could also say, "lo mismo para ti" for more emphasis.

Dialogue:

Margarita: Buena suerte en el examen.

Good luck on the test.

Pedro: ¡Igualmente!

Same to you!

Now Practice: ¡Igualmente!

Repeat Aloud 3 times slowly to practice

52. Voy a dormir—I'm going to sleep

   Dialogue:

   Margarita: Te ves cansado.

   You look tired.

   Pedro: Si, estoy candsado. Voy a dormir ahora.

   Yes, I am tired. I'm going to sleep now.

   Now Practice: Voy a dormir

   Repeat Aloud 3 times slowly to practice

53. ¿Vas a dormir?—Are you going to sleep?

   Dialogue:

   Margarita: ¿Te veré después?

   Will I see you later?

   Pedro: Depende. ¿Cuando vas a dormir?

   It depends. When are you going to sleep?

   Now Practice: ¿Vas a dormir?

   Repeat Aloud 3 times slowly to practice

54. desayunar —to have breakfast
   (NOTE: this translates to, "to breakfast," in English, we'd always use a helping verb like, "to have breakfast," but it's not necessary in Spanish. They have a verb form of breakfast.)

   Dialogue:

   Margarita: ¿Quieres desayunar juntos mañana?

   Do you want to have breakfast together tomorrow?

   Pedro: ¡Si, Por supuesto! Eso estaría bien.

   Yes sure. That would be nice.

   Now Practice: desayunar

55. almorzar —to have lunch
(NOTE: see how this is the same as the verb for breakfast? You don't need to use the helping verb "tener," because almorzar is already a verb.)

Dialogue:

Margarita: ¿Que haces el miércoless?

What are you doing on Wednesday?

Pedro: Nada. Almorcemos el miércoles.

Nothing. Let's get lunch on Wednesday.

Now Practice: almorzar

Repeat Aloud 3 times slowly to practice

56. Cenar—to have dinner

Dialogue:

Margarita: ¿A qué hora quieres cenar?

What time do you want to have dinner?

Pedro: A las seis y media. ¿Esta bien?

At 6:30. Is that okay?

Now Practice: Cenar

Repeat Aloud 3 times slowly to practice

57. Tomar un bocadillo—have a snack
(Bocadillo usually means "sandwich," but can be used to simply mean, "snack." You could also say aperitivo," which means something like "appetizer" but can also be understood as, "snack." You can also just simply say, "comer algo." This is a more common way to express it, and it simply means, "to eat something," but a snack is implied.")

Dialogue:

Margarita: Tengo mucha hambre.

I am so hungry.

Pedro: Quizas debes Tomar un bocadillo.

Maybe you should have a snack.

Now Practice: Fare uno sputino

Repeat Aloud 3 times slowly to practice

58. Sì, por favor—yes, please

(You can also say, "si gracias," which translates to Yes, Thanks!)

Dialogue:

Margarita: Quieres un café?

Do you want a coffee?

Pedro: Sì, por favor.

Yes, please!

Now Practice: Sì, por favor.

Repeat Aloud 3 times slowly to practice

59. No, gracias—No, thanks

Dialogue:

Margarita: Quieres mas?

Do you want more?

Pedro: No, gracias.

No, thank you.

Now Practice: No, gracias

Repeat Aloud 3 times slowly to practice

60. Muchos gracias —Thank you so much!

(NOTE: this translates to "many thank you's" and is a very common way of thanking someone profusely or when a simple "gracias," is not sufficient.)

Dialogue:

Margarita: Te olvidaste tu celular. Lo agarré por ti.

You forgot your phone. I grabbed it for you.

Pedro: ¡Oh! ¡Muchas gracias Margarita!

Oh, thank you so much, Margarita!

Now Practice: Muchos gracias

Repeat Aloud 3 times slowly to practice

---

61. Llegar tarde—to be late

Dialogue:

Margarita: ¿A qué hora terminas tu trabajo?

What time do you finish work?

Pedro: A las cinco, pero llegaré tarde.

At five, but I'll be late.

Now Practice: Llegar tarde

Repeat Aloud 3 times slowly to practice

---

62. ¡Rápido!—Quickly!
(NOTE: usually you'll want to use a "por favor," or "gracias," to soften this command. It can sound a bit rude if you say it someone you don't know well without "please" or "thank you.")

Dialogue:

Margarita: Tengo que parar en la tienda antes de la cena.

I have to stop at the store before dinner.

Pedro: ¡Rápido, por favor! Tengo hambre.

Quickly, please! I'm hungry.

Now Practice: ¡Rápido!

Repeat Aloud 3 times slowly to practice

---

63. En un poco—in a little bit

(Note: use this like, "see you in a little bit.")

Dialogue:

Margarita: Voy a visitar a mi abuela ahora.

I'm going to visit my grandma now.

Pedro: Vale. Te veré en un poco.

Okay. I'll see you in a bit.

Now Practice: En un poco

Repeat Aloud 3 times slowly to practice

---

64. ¡Hasta mañana! —See you tomorrow

(Note: this translates to, "to tomorrow," or "until tomorrow," but is commonly understood to mean: "see you tomorrow.")

Dialogue:

Margarita: Voy a dormir ahora.

I'm going to sleep now.

Pedro: Vale. ¡Hasta mañana!

Okay. See you tomorrow!

Now Practice: ¡Hasta mañana!

Repeat Aloud 3 times slowly to practice

---

65. Me voy a casa—I'm going home

Dialogue:

Margarita: ¿Cuándo quieres estudiar juntos?

When do you want to study together?

Pedro: En unas horas. Me voy a casa a dormir una siesta ahora.

In a few hours. I'm going home for a nap now.

Now Practice: Me voy a casa

Repeat Aloud 3 times slowly to practice

---

66. Un momento –Just one moment
(Note: although this literally just translates to, "A moment," it's not too brisk or rude to say by itself (especially if you say it with a smile). However, for an even better effect, add a "gracias" to the end of it. Or you could also say, "solo un momento.")

Dialogue:

Margarita: ¿Puedes hablar ahora?

Can you talk now?

Pedro: Un momento, estoy al teléfono.

Just a moment, I'm on the phone.

Now Practice: Un momento

Repeat Aloud 3 times slowly to practice

---

67. ¡Adios, hasta proxima!—goodbye, see you next time

Dialogue:

Margarita: ¡La comida fue deliciosa! ¡Bye bye!

The meal was delicious! Bye bye!

Waiter in Restaurant: ¡Adios! Hasta Próximo. ¡Muchas gracias!

Goodbye! See you next time. Thank you so much!

Now Practice: ¡Adios, hasta proxima!

Repeat Aloud 3 times slowly to practice

---

68. ¿Cuál es tu trabajo?—What's your job?

(Note: this directly translates to, "what work do you do?" but it can also mean, "what's your job?")

Dialogue:

Margarita: ¿Cuál es tu trabajo?

What's your new job?

Pedro: Trabajo en ventas, ahora.

I work in sales now.

Now Practice: ¿Cuál es tu trabajo?

Repeat Aloud 3 times slowly to practice

---

69. ¿Tiene...?—do you have?

(NOTE: you can use this in a shop or at a restaurant when you're looking for something specific.)

Dialogue:

Margarita: ¿Tienes un boligrafo?

Got a pen?

Pedro: No. Solo un lápiz.

No, only a pencil.

Now Practice: ¿Tiene...?

Repeat Aloud 3 times slowly to practice

---

70. Sólo estoy mirando—I'm just looking
(NOTE: say this when you're in a shop if they're pestering you and you just want to have a look around. It's always nice to add a gracias at the end.)

Dialogue:

Cashier: ¿Puedo ayudarte a encontrar algo?

Can I help you find something?

Pedro: No, gracias. Sólo estoy mirando

No thanks, I'm just looking.

Now Practice: Sólo estoy mirando

Repeat Aloud 3 times slowly to practice

---

71. ¿Cuanto cuesta? –how much does it cost?

Dialogue:

Margarita: ¿Cuánto cuesta una cerveza?

How much does a beer cost?

Waiter: Depende del tipo de cerveza.

It depends on the type of beer.

Now Practice: ¿Cuanto cuesta?

Repeat Aloud 3 times slowly to practice

---

72. ¿Cuánto me hace pagar?—How much do you want for this?

(NOTE: Another more sophisticated way of asking how much something costs.)

Dialogue:

Margarita: ¿Cuánto me hace pagar?

How much do you want for this?

Cashier: Solo veinte dólares, gracias.

Only $20.

Now Practice: ¿Cuánto me hace pagar?

73. Demasiado caro—That's too expensive!

Dialogue:

Margarita: ¿Vente Dólares? Eso es demasiado caro

Twenty dollars? That's too expensive!

Cashier: Lo siento, eso es mi mejor oferta.

Sorry, that's my best offer.

Now Practice: Demasiado caro

Repeat Aloud 3 times slowly to practice

74. Eso es barato —that's cheap!

Dialogue:

Cashier: Te daré dos por el precio de uno.

I'll give you two for the price of one.

Pedro: ¡Eso es barato!

That's cheap!

Now Practice: Eso es barato

Repeat Aloud 3 times slowly to practice

75. ¿Acepta tarjetas?—do you accept credit cards?

(You can also say "tarjetas de credito" to be more specific.)

Dialogue:

Pedro: ¿Acepta tarjetas?

Do you take credit cards?

Cashier: Lo siento, sólo en efectivo.

Sorry, cash only.

Now Practice: ¿Acepta tarjetas?

Repeat Aloud 3 times slowly to practice

76. ¿Perdón, donde está el baño?—Excuse me, Where is the bathroom?

Dialogue:

Pedro: ¿Perdón, donde está el baño?

Do you take credit cards?

Waiter: Sigue derecho, y a la izquierda.

Straight ahead and to the left.

Now Practice: ¿Perdón, donde está el baño?

Repeat Aloud 3 times slowly to practice

77. ¿Cuánto dura el viaje?—How long is the journey

(how long does it take?) Note: you can use this for different types of situations. If you're asking for directions and wanting to know how long it will take you to get there, you can say, "¿Cuánto dura el viaje?" Similarly, you can say that if you're on a train or bus and want to know how long the trip is going to take.)

Dialogue:

Pedro: ¿Cuánto dura el viaje?

How long is the journey?

Attendant: Alrededor de dos horas

About two hours.

Now Practice: ¿Cuánto dura el viaje?

Repeat Aloud 3 times slowly to practice

78. El clima es bueno—the weather is good

Dialogue:

Pedro: ¿Quieres ir al parque mañana?

Do you want to go to the park tomorrow?

Margarita: Por su puesto, si el clima es bueno.

Sure, if the weather is nice.

Now Practice: El clima es bueno

Repeat Aloud 3 times slowly to practice

79. ¿Me permite?—May I?

(NOTE: this translates to something like, "Permission?" Use it the way we'd use "May I?" in English. For example, if you knock on a door, you could say: "¿Me permite?" for "May I come in?" Or if you're in a shop and want to take a closer look at something and pick it up, you could say, "¿Me permite?"

Dialogue:

Pedro: ¿Hay alguien sentado aquí?

Is anyone sitting here?

Margarita: No, nadie.

No, nobdody.

Pedro: ¿Me permite?

May I?

Now Practice: ¿Me permite?

Repeat Aloud 3 times slowly to practice

---

80. Lo siento—I'm sorry

    Dialogue:

    Pedro: Olvidaste a comprar leche.

    You forgot to buy milk.

    Margarita: Lo siento, lo compraré mañana.

    I'm sorry, I'll buy it tomorrow.

    Now Practice: Lo siento

    Repeat Aloud 3 times slowly to practice

---

81. ¿Hablas ingles?—do you speak English?

    Dialogue:

    Pedro: Perdon, ¿hablas Ingles?

    Excuse me, do you speak English?

    Attendant: No, no lo hablo. Lo siento.

    No I don't, I'm sorry.

    Now Practice: ¿Hablas ingles?

    Repeat Aloud 3 times slowly to practice

---

82. Sí, un poco—yes, a little.

    Dialogue:

Pedro: Perdon, ¿Hablas ingles?

Excuse me, do you speak English?

Attendant: Si, un poco.

Yes, a little.

Now Practice: Sì, un poco

Repeat Aloud 3 times slowly to practice

83. No, lo siento. No hablo Ingles—No I'm sorry, I do not speak English.

(Note: You may also hear: "No, lo siento. No lo hablo." as a direct response which just means, "I'm sorry I don't speak it.")

Dialogue:

Pedro: Perdón, ¿hablas Ingles?

Excuse me, do you speak English?

Attendant: No, lo siento. No hablo Ingles.

No, I'm sorry, I don't speak English.

Now Practice: No, lo siento. No hablo Ingles.

Repeat Aloud 3 times slowly to practice

84. No entiendo—I don't understand

(Note: you could also say, "no lo veo" which actually translates to "I don't see" but is used the same way we use, "I don't understand.")

Dialogue:

Tourist: No entiendo que dices.

I don't understand what you're saying

Pedro: Esta bien. Hablaré más despacio.

It's okay, I'll speak more slowly.

Now Practice: No entiendo

Repeat Aloud 3 times slowly to practice

85. Tiene sentido--That makes sense

(NOTE: this translates to: "it has sense." It wouldn't be correct to say, "hacer senso," like we'd say "make sense" in English.)

Dialogue:

Margarita: Voy a ir a casa antes de que nos encontremos.

I'm going to go home before we meet up.

Pedro: Tiene sentido. Te veré en un poco.

That makes sense, I'll see you in a bit.

Now Practice: Tiene sentido

Repeat Aloud 3 times slowly to practice

---

86. No se como se dice en Español—I don't know how to say it in Spanish

Dialogue:

Attendant: ¿Puedo ayudarte?

May I help you?

Pedro: Estoy en busca de algo, pero no sé cómo se dice en español.

I'm looking for something, but I don't know how to say it in Spanish.

Now Practice: No sé cómo se dice en español

Repeat Aloud 3 times slowly to practice

---

87. ¿Como se dice_____ en español? --How do you say ___ in Spanish?

Dialogue:

Pedro: ¿Como se dice, "Cat" en español?

How do you say, "Cat" in Spanish?

Margarita: Gatto. Gatto es la palabra para "cat."

Gatto. Gatto is the word for cat.

Now Practice: ¿Como se dice _____ en español?

Repeat Aloud 3 times slowly to practice

---

88. Non tiene sentido—It doesn't make sense

Dialogue:

Pedro: Non tiene sentido. ¿Por qué no me llamo Catarina?

It doesn't make sense. Why didn't Catarina call me?

Margarita: Tal vez ella sólo está ocupada.

Maybe she's just busy.

Now Practice: Non tiene sentido

Repeat Aloud 3 times slowly to practice

89. ¿Que quieres decir con…?—What do you mean by…?

(NOTE: this is a very useful phrase when you're speaking with a native Spanish speaker and you don't understand an expression they've used. There are many colorful idioms in the Spanish language and some of them vary by region, so you may hear someone say something that makes no sense to you. You can use this phrase to ask them to explain it to you.)

Dialogue:

Margarita: ¿Qué quieres decir con "tomando el pelo?"

What do you mean by the phrase, "pulling my leg?"

Pedro: Significa que estoy haciendo una broma.

It means I'm making a joke.

Now Practice: ¿Qué quieres decir con…?—

Repeat Aloud 3 times slowly to practice

90. que hacer cola—to wait in line

Dialogue:

Margarita: ¿Tiene un baño?

Do they have a bathroom?

Pedro: Si, pero necesitas que hacer cola.

Yes, but you have to wait in line.

Now Practice: que hacer cola

Repeat Aloud 3 times slowly to practice

91. girar a la derecha—turn right

Dialogue:

Margarita: Ahora, ¿dónde voy?

Now where do I go?

Pedro: Gire a la derecha en la próxima calle.

Turn right on the next street.

Now Practice: girar a la derecha

Repeat Aloud 3 times slowly to practice

92. girar a la izquierda—turn left

Dialogue:

Margarita: Ahora, ¿dónde voy?

Now where do I go?

Pedro: Gire izquierda en la próxima calle.

Turn left on the next street.

Now Practice: girar a la izquierda

Repeat Aloud 3 times slowly to practice

93. Siga recta—go straight

Dialogue:

Margarita: Siga recta.

Go straight.

Pedro: Lo sé, gracias.

I know, thanks.

Now Practice: Siga recta

Repeat Aloud 3 times slowly to practice

94. ve por este camino —go this way

Dialogue:

Margarita: No ve por este camino.

Don't go this way.

Pedro: ¿Por que no?

Why not?

Now Practice: ve por este camino

Repeat Aloud 3 times slowly to practice

---

95. dar la vuelta—go back/turn around

    Dialogue:

    Margarita: ¡Date vuelta!

    Go back.

    Pedro: ¿He pasado la entrada?

    Did I pass the entrance?

    Now Practice: dar la vuelta

    Repeat Aloud 3 times slowly to practice

96. Para aquí—stop here

    Dialogue:

    Margarita: ¿Dónde me paro?

    Where should I stop?

    Pedro: Para aquí, por favor.

    Stop here please.

    Now Practice: Para aquí

    Repeat Aloud 3 times slowly to practice

---

97. Perdóname —Excuse me

(you can also use this as a more casual way of saying sorry. In public with people you don't know, it's probably more correct to say, "perdóname," than "lo siento.")

Dialogue:

Margarita: Perdóname, ¿Puedo poner mi bolso aquí?

Excuse me, can I put my bag here?

Attendant: Si, está bien.

Yes, that's fine.

Now Practice: Perdóname

Repeat Aloud 3 times slowly to practice

---

98. ¿Hay habitaciones libres?—Do you have any vacant rooms?

Dialogue:

Margarita: ¿Hay habitaciones libres?

Do you have any vacant rooms?

Attendant: Si, pero solo tenemos uno más.

Yes we only have one left.

Now Practice: ¿Hay habitaciones libres?

Repeat Aloud 3 times slowly to practice

---

99. ¿Qué quieres hacer?—What do you want to do?

Dialogue:

Margarita: ¿Qué quieres hacer este noche?

What do you want to do tonight?

Pedro: Vamos al cine.

Let's go to the movies.

Now Practice: ¿Qué quieres hacer?

Repeat Aloud 3 times slowly to practice

---

100. Donde debemos ir?—Where should we go?

Dialogue:

Margarita: ¿Donde debemos ir almorzar?

Where do you want to go for lunch?

Pedro: Vamos al nuevo restaurante asiático.

Let's go to that new Asian restaurant.

Now Practice: Donde debemos ir?

Repeat Aloud 3 times slowly to practice

---

101. Encontrémonos —Let's meet

(there are many ways to say this. You could also say, "reunamonos," or, "nos vemos.")

Dialogue:

Margarita: ¿Cuáles son tus planes para mañana?

What are your plans for tomorrow?

Pedro: No tengo nada planeado. Encontrémonos para almorzar.

I have nothing planned. Let's meet for lunch.

Now Practice: Encontrémonos

Repeat Aloud 3 times slowly to practice

102. ¿Quieres comer?—Do you want to eat?

Dialogue:

Margarita: ¿Quieres comer?

Do you want to eat?

Pedro: ¡Si! ¡Tengo mucha hambre!

Yes! I'm so hungry!

Now Practice: ¿Quieres comer?

Repeat Aloud 3 times slowly to practice

103. Vamos a comer—Let's go eat

Dialogue:

Margarita: Vamos a comer

Let's go eat.

Pedro: Vale. ¿Donde quiere comer?

Okay. Where do you want to go?

Now Practice: Vamos a comer

Repeat Aloud 3 times slowly to practice

104. Vamos a salir—Let's go out

(NOTE: you can use this in terms of going out to eat, or going out drinking etc.)

Dialogue:

Margarita: Quiero bailar.

I want to dance.

Pedro: Vale. ¡Vamos a salir!

Okay. Let's go out.

Now Practice: Vamos a salir

Repeat Aloud 3 times slowly to practice

---

105. ¿que recomiendas?—what do you recommend?

Dialogue:

Margarita: Nunca he estado aquí. ¿Que recomiendas?

I've never been here. What do you recommend?

Pedro: El pollo es delicioso.

The chicken is delicious!

Now Practice: ¿que recomiendas?

Repeat Aloud 3 times slowly to practice

---

106. ¿Qué quieres pedir?—What do you want (to order)

(Note: this translates to something like, "What will you make?" This is a common way of asking for someone's order. In a restaurant, you may commonly hear, "¿Qué quieres pedir?" or simply, "¿Que pides?" from the waiter or the employee at the counter.)

Dialogue:

Attendant: ¿Qué quieres pedir?

What do you want to order?

Pedro: No estamos listos todavía. Unos minutos más por favor.

We're not ready yet. A few more minutes please.

Now Practice: ¿Qué quieres pedir?

Repeat Aloud 3 times slowly to practice

---

107. ¿Puedo ordenar?—Can I order?

(Note: you can also say, "Me pones un…" this is more of a colloquial way of ordering.)

Dialogue:

Attendant: ¿Qué quieres pedir?

What do you want to order?

Pedro: Me pones dos cervezas para empezar.

Can I order two beers to start?

Now Practice: ¿Puedo ordenar?

Repeat Aloud 3 times slowly to practice

108. Quiero más —I want more

(NOTE: it's always nice to add a "por favor," on the end of this.)

Dialogue:

Pedro: ¿Como esta tu comida?

How's your meal?

Margarita: ¡Delicioso! Quiero más.

Delicious! I want more.

Now Practice: Quiero más

Repeat Aloud 3 times slowly to practice

109. Quiero menos—I want less

Dialogue:

Pedro: Cuanta ensalada quieres?

How much salad do you want?

Margarita: Quiero menos. Esto es demasiado.

I want less. This is too much.

Now Practice: Quiero menos

Repeat Aloud 3 times slowly to practice

110. ¿Te gusta?—Do you like it?

Dialogue:

Pedro: ¿Te gusta el vino?

Do you like the wine?

Margarita: No mucho. Esta demasiado dulce.

Not very much. It's too sweet.

Now Practice: ¿Te gusta?

Repeat Aloud 3 times slowly to practice

---

111. ¡Me gusta mucho!—I like it a lot!

Dialogue:

Pedro: ¿Qué piensas de esto canción?

What do you think of this song?

Margarita: ¡Me gusta mucho!

I like it a lot!

Now Practice ¡Me gusta mucho!

Repeat Aloud 3 times slowly to practice

---

112. Tengo una reservacion—I have a reservation

Dialogue:

Attendant: ¿Le puedo ayudar, por favor?

May I help you?

Margarita: Si, tengo una reservacion.

Yes, I have a reservation.

Now Practice Tengo una reservacion

Repeat Aloud 3 times slowly to practice

---

113. ¿Puedes darme un descuento? —can you give me a discount?

(Note: Don't be afraid to use this one. In Hispanic culture, it's very common to ask for a deal. If you're a foreigner, they may be less inclined to give you one, but if you can ask in Spanish, they might be impressed enough to give you one after all.)

Dialogue:

Attendant: Tu total llega a cincuenta y cinco dólares.

Your total comes to fifty-five euros.

Margarita: ¿Puedes darme un descuento?

Can you give me a discount?

Now Practice ¿Puedes darme un descuento?

114. Lo compraré—I'll take it

(Note: although the verb "comprar" refers to buying something, you can also use this expression the way we sometimes use the English expression, "I'll take it." For example, if something turns out better than you expected, you could say: "Lo compro!")

Dialogue:

Attendant: Tenemos uno en tu tamaño.

We have one in your size.

Margarita: ¡Fantástico! ¡Lo comprare!

Great! I'll take it!

Now Practice Lo compraré

Repeat Aloud 3 times slowly to practice

115. ¿Algo más?—Anything else?

(This might seem a bit rude but it's all in the delivery. Say it with a smile and it will be perfectly normal. You will probably hear this when you buy something and it means, "Anything else?")

Dialogue:

Attendant: ¿Algo más?

Anything else?

Margarita: No, gracias. Solo esto.

No thank you, only this.

Now Practice: ¿Algo más?

Repeat Aloud 3 times slowly to practice

116. Nada más, gracias—Nothing else, Thanks.

Dialogue:

Attendant: ¿Algo más?

Anything else?

Margarita: Nada más, gracias.

Nothing else, thanks.

Now Practice Nada más, gracias

Repeat Aloud 3 times slowly to practice

---

117. Otro—another

(Note: you should add, por favor or gracias to the end of this. This is commonly used in restaurants or bars to order another of whatever you're eating/drinking.)

Dialogue:

Attendant: ¿Te gustaría otra cerveza, señorita?

Would you like another beer, ma'am?

Margarita: Si, otra gracias.

Yes, another one thanks.

Now Practice: otro

Repeat Aloud 3 times slowly to practice

---

118. Gracias de todos modos—thanks anyway

(NOTE: there are many ways to say this. "Gracias de todos modos" is probably the most common, but you will also hear, "gracias de cualquier manera," and "gracias igual." These all essentially mean the same thing, "Thanks anyway," or "thank you just the same." Etc.)

Dialogue:

Attendant: ¿Te gustaría otra copa de vino, señor?

Would you like another glass of wine, sir?

Pedro: No, pero gracias de todos modos.

No but thanks anyway.

Now Practice: Gracias de todos modos

Repeat Aloud 3 times slowly to practice

---

119. Ir de compras—to do the shopping (to go shopping)

(This doesn't exactly translate to English because it roughly means something like, "to go of the purchases," but nonetheless, it's how you'd say, "to shop" or "to go shopping." Do not use, "Ir comprando" as this is not correct. You could also use, "Salir de compras," or "Hacer compras.")

Dialogue:

Pedro: ¿Quieres ir de compras con mi hermana y yo?

Do you want to go shopping with my sister and I?

Margarita: Desafortunadamente no puedo. Estoy en el trabajo.

Unfortunately I can't. I'm at work.

Now Practice Ir de compras

Repeat Aloud 3 times slowly to practice

120. Hacer amigos—to make friends with

Dialogue:

Margarita: Debes hacer amigos con mi prima, Sofia.

You should be friends with my cousin Sofia.

Pedro: Bueno, quiero conocerla.

Yes, I want to meet her.

Now Practice Hacer amigos

Repeat Aloud 3 times slowly to practice

121. Hacer un lio—to make a mess

Dialogue:

Margarita: Traté de hornear un pastel.

I tried to bake a cake.

Pedro: JaJaJa. Hiciste un lío.

Hahaha. You made a mess.

Now Practice Hacer un lio

Repeat Aloud 3 times slowly to practice

122. Volver loco—to make someone crazy (to drive someone crazy)

Dialogue:

Margarita: A veces, mi madre me vuelve loco.

Sometimes my mom drives me crazy.

Pedro: Jajaja. ¿Que hizo ella esta vez?

Hahaha. What did she do this time?

Now Practice Volver loco

123. Hacer sentir mal—to make (someone) feel bad

Dialogue:

Margarita: ¡Pedro! Olvidaste mi cumpleaños.

Pedro! You forgot my birthday!

Pedro: ¡Oh no! Lo siento. Eso me hace sentir mal.

Oh no! I'm sorry. That makes me feel bad.

Now Practice Hacer sentir mal

Repeat Aloud 3 times slowly to practice

124. Me lo estoy pasando bien—I'm having a good time

Dialogue:

Margarita: ¿Estas disfrutando la fiesta?

Are you enjoying the party?

Pedro: Si. Me lo estoy pasando bien.

Yes. I'm having a good time.

Now Practice Me lo estoy pasando bien.

Repeat Aloud 3 times slowly to practice

125. Mesa para dos—a table for two,

(Note: it's always nice to add a "gracias" or "por favor" on to the end of this to make it more polite.)

Dialogue:

Attendant: ¿Como puedo ayudarle?

How can I help you?

Pedro: Mesa para dos, por favor.

A table for two please.

Now Practice Mesa para dos

Repeat Aloud 3 times slowly to practice

126. Tú decides—You decide

Dialogue:

Margarita: ¿Que debemos ordenar para aperitivo?

What should we order for an appetizer?

Pedro: Tú decides

You decide.

Now Practice Tú decides

Repeat Aloud 3 times slowly to practice

127. ¿Que hora es?—what time is it?

Dialogue:

Margarita: ¿Qué hora es ahora?

What time is it now?

Pedro: Solo son las tres. Todavía tenemos tiempo.

Only three o'clock. We still have time.

Now Practice: ¿Qué hora es ahora?

Repeat Aloud 3 times slowly to practice

128. ¿Come llego alli?—How can I get there?

Dialogue:

Margarita: ¿Como llego a la biblioteca?

How do I get to the library?

Pedro: Te mostraré el camino

I'll show you the way.

Now Practice: ¿Come llego alli?

Repeat Aloud 3 times slowly to practice

129. No me siento bien—I don't feel well

Dialogue:

Margarita: No me siento bien.

I don't feel well.

Pedro: Oh no. ¿Qué pasa?

Oh no. What's wrong?

Now Practice: No me siento bien

Repeat Aloud 3 times slowly to practice

130. ¿Puedo preguntarte algo? –Can I ask you something?

Dialogue:

Margarita: ¿Puedo preguntarte algo?

Can I ask you something?

Pedro: ¡Sí, por su puesto! ¿Qué pasa?

Yes of course. What's up?

Now Practice: ¿Puedo preguntarte algo?

Repeat Aloud 3 times slowly to practice

131. enojarse—to get angry

Dialogue:

Margarita: ¿Tu jefe no volvió a trabajar hoy?

Your boss didn't come to work again today?

Pedro: No. Todavia no. Me estoy enojando.

No. Still no. I'm getting angry.

Now Practice: enojarse

Repeat Aloud 3 times slowly to practice

132. estar cansado—to be tired

Dialogue:

Margarita: ¿Debemos salir esta noche?

Should we go out tonight?

Pedro: No se…Estoy cansado.

I don't know…I'm tired.

Now Practice: estar cansado

Repeat Aloud 3 times slowly to practice

133. En mi opinión —in my opinion

Dialogue:

Margarita: ¿Fue buena, la película?

Was the movie good?

Pedro: En mi opinión, sí.

In my opinion, yes.

Now Practice: En mi opinión

Repeat Aloud 3 times slowly to practice

---

134. me sacar de quicio —to get on my nerves

(There are multiple ways to say this phrase. "me sacas de quicio," is just one of them. You could also say, "me pones los nervios de punta," (you put my nerves on edge), or "me molestas," you bother me.)

Dialogue:

Margarita: Mi jefe me saca de quicio.

My boss drives me crazy.

Pedro: Si, eres fastidioso.

In my opinion, yes.

Now Practice: me sacar de quicio

Repeat Aloud 3 times slowly to practice

---

135. perdedor—a loser

(This is used to describe someone that has bad luck or always seems to be on the losing end.)

Dialogue:

Pedro: Perdí una fortuna en el casino.

I lost a fortune in the casino.

Margarita: Eres perdedor.

You're a loser.

Now Practice: perdedor

Repeat Aloud 3 times slowly to practice

---

136. Quizás—maybe

(You can also say "tal vez," both are equally acceptable ways of saying "maybe.")

Dialogue:

Pedro: ¿Vienes a la fiesta más tarde?

Are you coming to the party later?

Margarita: Quizás. Depende si termino mi trabajo.

Maybe. It depends if I finish my work.

Now Practice: Quizás

Repeat Aloud 3 times slowly to practice

137. Indudablemente—doubtless/without a doubt

(You could also say, "sin duda," for "without a doubt," or "indudable.")

Dialogue:

Pedro: ¿A qué hora terminas tu trabajo?

What time do you get off work?

Margarita: A las cinco, pero indudablemente será más tarde.

At five but doubtless it'll be later.

Now Practice: Indudablemente

Repeat Aloud 3 times slowly to practice

138. ¿Me puedes ayudar?—can you help me?

Dialogue:

Pedro: ¿Me puedes ayudar?

Can you help me?

Margarita: ¿Por su puesto, que necesitas?

Sure, what do you need?

Now Practice: ¿Me puedes ayudar?

Repeat Aloud 3 times slowly to practice

139. te ayudare—I'll help you

Dialogue:

Margarita: Tengo mucho para hacer antes de lleguen mis padres.

I have so much to do before my parents arrive.

Pedro: No te preocupas, te ayudare.

Don't worry, I'll help you.

Now Practice: te ayudare

Repeat Aloud 3 times slowly to practice

---

140. Necesito ayuda —I need help

Dialogue:

Margarita: Necesito ayuda con algo.

I need help with something.

Pedro: Bueno, ¿Qué pasa?

Okay, what's up?

Now Practice: Necesito ayuda

Repeat Aloud 3 times slowly to practice

---

141. Gracias por tu ayuda—Thank you for your help

Dialogue:

Attendant: ¿Hay algo más en que puedo ayudarte?

Is there anything else I can help you with?

Pedro: No, nada más. Gracias por tu ayuda

No nothing else. Thanks for your help.

Now Practice: Gracias por tu ayuda

Repeat Aloud 3 times slowly to practice

---

142. ¿Puedo ayudarte?—May I help you?

Dialogue:

Attendant: ¿Puedo ayudarte?

Is there anything else I can help you with?

Pedro: Si, estoy buscando la estación de tren.

Yes, I'm looking for the train station.

Now Practice: ¿Puedo ayudarte?

Repeat Aloud 3 times slowly to practice

143. ¡Absolutamente!—Absolutely!

Dialogue:

Margarita: Llegaras a tiempo?

Will you arrive on time?

Pedro: ¡Absolutamente! Vengo ahora.

Absolutelly! I'm coming now.

Now Practice: ¡Absolutamente!

Repeat Aloud 3 times slowly to practice

---

144. De todos modos—anyway/doesn't matter

(there are many ways of saying this. You could say, "de todas maneras," or "de todas formas." These all mean the same thing more or less. Sometimes it may also be appropriate to simply say, "no importa," in a situation where you'd say, "anyways" or "it doesn't matter."

Dialogue:

Margarita: No voy a la fiesta de Navidad esta noche.

I'm not going to the Christmas party tonight.

Pedro: Que lastima, pero todavía voy de todos modos.

What a shame, but I'm still going anyway.

Now Practice: De todos modos

Repeat Aloud 3 times slowly to practice

---

145. Creo que—I think that

(Note: This translates more directly to, "I believe," but it's more often used when we'd use, "I think." You wouldn't usually use the verb pensar when expressing an opinion. You can also say, "me parace," which more directly translates to, "it seems to me...")

Dialogue:

Margarita: Creo que es hora de irse.

I think it's time to leave.

Pedro: ¿Por qué? ¿Qué pasa?

Why? What's wrong?

Now Practice: Creo que

Repeat Aloud 3 times slowly to practice

---

146. Por Dios—Please!/ For mercy's sake

(Note: This translates to, "For God!" and is a very common expression especially in the middle-aged and older crowd. You can use it the way we'd use, "For goodness sake," or "Lord have mercy!")

Dialogue:

Margarita: Todavía no sé por qué dijiste eso.

I still don't know why you said that.

Pedro: ¡Por Dios! Déjalo ir.

For heaven's sake, let it go.

Now Practice: Por Dios

Repeat Aloud 3 times slowly to practice

---

147. Pasar el rato—to hang out/go out

(Note: this directly translates roughly to, "to pass a little while," and this is a very common expression to use when you're spending time with people. It can be used in a wide variety of situations much like the phrase, "hanging out," in English. It can also be used for, "going out with friends.")

Dialogue:

Margarita: ¿Quieres pasar el rato?

Do you want to hang out?

Pedro: ¡Claro! ¿Qué quieres hacer?

Sure! What do you want to do?

Now Practice: pasar el rato

Repeat Aloud 3 times slowly to practice

---

148. Déjalo ir—let it go

(this translates to, "leave it go," and can be likened to the English phrases: Let it go, or Leave it be.")

Dialogue:

Margarita: ¿Debo decirle algo a él?

Should I say something to him?

Pedro: No, déjalo ir.

No, just let it go.

Now Practice: Déjalo ir

Repeat Aloud 3 times slowly to practice

---

149. ¿Qué estás buscando? –what are you looking for?

Dialogue:

Margarita: ¿Qué estás buscando?

What are you looking for?

Pedro: Mi celular. Lo perdí.

My cell phone. I lost it.

Now Practice: ¿Qué estás buscando?

Repeat Aloud 3 times slowly to practice

---

150. Dar por sentado—take for granted

(This doesn't have a direct translation, but it's something like, "give for seated.")

Dialogue:

Margarita: El clima es muy agradable.

The weather is so nice!

Pedro: Sí lo es. No lo demos por sentado

Yes, it is. Let's not take it for granted.

Now Practice: Dar por sentado

Repeat Aloud 3 times slowly to practice

---

151. Hacer un favor—to do a favor

Dialogue:

Margarita: ¿Me puedes hacer un favor?

Can you do me a favor?

Pedro: ¡Claro! ¿Como puedo ayudar?

Of course! How can I help?

Now Practice: Hacer un favor

Repeat Aloud 3 times slowly to practice

---

152. seguir adelante—go ahead

(NOTE: don't use this in a situation where you're politely trying to tell someone they can go in front of you. If you're in line and want to let someone in front of you, say "por favor." Use "seguir adelante" when you're telling someone to get started with something. For example, if someone tells you they need to tell you something, you can say: "Sigue adelante." Or if someone is in the middle of something, you can say, "continua," to ask them to keep going.

Dialogue:

Margarita: ¿Puedo decirte algo?

Can I tell you something?

Pedro: Si, seguir adelante.

Yes, go head.

Now Practice: seguir adelante

Repeat Aloud 3 times slowly to practice

---

153. sorprender—to surprise

Dialogue:

Margarita: ¿Qué sabor de helado quieres?

What flavor of ice cream do you want?

Pedro: Sorpréndeme.

Surprise me.

Now Practice: sorprender

Repeat Aloud 3 times slowly to practice

---

154. tener calor—to be warm

Dialogue:

Margarita: ¿Quieres una chaqueta?

Do you want a jacket?

Pedro: No gracias. Tengo mucho calor.

No thanks. I'm very warm.

Now Practice: tener calor

Repeat Aloud 3 times slowly to practice

---

155. hacer frio—to be cold
Dialogue:

Margarita: Hoy está haciendo mucho frio.

It's very cold today.

Pedro: Me gusta el clima frío.

I like the cold weather.

Now Practice: hacer frio

Repeat Aloud 3 times slowly to practice

---

156. pagar una visita—to pay someone a visit

(You can also simply use the verb, "visitar."

Dialogue:

Margarita: ¿Cuándo vas a pagar una visita a mi familia?

When are you going to pay my family a visit?

Pedro: Ojalá en unas semanas cuando tenga tiempo.

Hopefully in a few weeks when I have time.

Now Practice: pagar una visita

Repeat Aloud 3 times slowly to practice

---

157. ser gracioso—to be funny

Dialogue:

Margarita: ¿Te hice reir?

Did I make you laugh?

Pedro: Si. Eres muy gracioso a veces.

Yes. You are very funny sometimes.

Now Practice: ser gracioso

Repeat Aloud 3 times slowly to practice

---

158. hacer una broma—make a joke

Dialogue:

Margarita: ¿Realmente vas a dejar tu trabajo?

Are you really going to quit your job?

Pedro: No. Solo estoy haciendo una broma.

No. I was only making a joke.

Now Practice: no hacer una broma

Repeat Aloud 3 times slowly to practice

---

159. llama a la policía—Call the police!

Dialogue:

Margarita: Creo que alguien robó mi bolso

I think someone stole my purse.

Pedro: ¿En serio? ¡Llama a la policía!

Seriously? Call the pólice!

Now Practice: llama a la policía

Repeat Aloud 3 times slowly to practice

---

160. Vete—Get out/Go!

(Note: This is more of a literal translation of "Get out," or "go." To say "get out of here" like the English expression, you can say, "vete," or "Fuera de aqui.")

Dialogue:

Margarita: Creo que hay una pelea en el bar.

I think there is a fight in the bar.

Pedro: Entonces, vete.

Then get out of there.

Now Practice: Vete

Repeat Aloud 3 times slowly to practice

---

161. estoy perdido —I'm lost

Dialogue:

Attendant: ¿Puedo ayudarle?

Can I help you?

Pedro: Si, creo que estoy perdido. Necesito instrucciones.

Yes, I think I'm lost. I need directions.

Now Practice: estoy perdido

Repeat Aloud 3 times slowly to practice

---

162. darle mis saludos —give my regards

(Note: this is more of an old-fashioned expression to give your regards or your best wishes to someone.)

Dialogue:

Margarita: Manana, voy a la boda de mi prima Catarina.

Tomorrow, I am going to my cousin Catarina's wedding.

Pedro: ¡Bueno! Dales mis saludos a ella y su esposo.

Great! Give my regards to her and her husband.

Now Practice: darle mis saludos

Repeat Aloud 3 times slowly to practice

---

163. Ten un buen viaje—have a good trip!

Dialogue:

Margarita: Te veré cuando vuelva de Europa.

I'll see you when I get back from Europe.

Pedro: ¡Nos vemos! Ten un buen viaje.

See you! Have a good trip.

Now Practice: Ten un buen viaje

Repeat Aloud 3 times slowly to practice

---

164. Hacer un tour—to take a tour

(Note: there are several ways to say this in Spanish. For a more casual situation, you could say, "dar una Vuelta," which basically means to walk around. If you simply wanted to walk around a place and not take a formal tour, you can use "dar una Vuelta." If you're referencing a more formal and organized tour, you could say, "hacer un tour," or "hacer un recorrido..")

Dialogue:

Margarita: Cuando lleguemos a Barcelona, ¿Debemos hacer un tour?

When we arrive in Spain, should we take a tour?

Pedro: No. Vamos a dar una vuelta del ciudad.

No, let's just walk around the city.

Now Practice: Hacer un tour

Repeat Aloud 3 times slowly to practice

---

165. hacer una fiesta—have a party

(NOTE: in English, we'd say "have a party," or nowadays, party is used as a verb, "Let's party!" but in Spanish, they use the verb to do or make, so it more directly translates to, "let's make a party." In some cases, you will also hear, "tener una fiesta," as well, which is more like the English equivalent.)

Dialogue:

Margarita: ¡Mi hermana y su novio se comprometieron!

My sister and her boyfriend got engaged!

Pedro: ¡Que exitante! Debemos hacer una fiesta para ellos.

How exciting! We should have a party for them.

Now Practice: hacer una fiesta

166. dar un paseo—take a walk

(Note: although in English we use the verb "to take," or "to go for," you wouldn't use "tomar" in Spanish. "dar un paseo," is the closest equivalent to "go for a walk.")

Dialogue:

Margarita: Damos un paseo.

Let's take a walk.

Pedro: Ok, Podemos ir al parque.

Ok, we can go to the park.

Now Practice: dar un paseo

Repeat Aloud 3 times slowly to practice

167. dar un regalo—to give a gift/present (NOTE: you can also use the verb "hacer," and say "hacer un regalo." Both are correct. "Hacer un regalo," might translate more to "to make a gift [of something]")

Dialogue:

Margarita: La semana próxima es mi cumpleaños. ¿Me darás un regalo?

Next week is my birthday. Are you going to give me a gift?

Pedro: Tal vez o tal vez no. Espera y verás.

Maybe, or maybe not. Wait and see.

Now Practice: dar un regalo

Repeat Aloud 3 times slowly to practice

168. hacer una llamada telefónica —make a phone call

(Note: it may be easier to simply say, "Hacer una llamada." Or you can also say, "llamar por telefono," which means, "to talk on the phone.")

Dialogue:

Margarita: Momentito. Necesito hacer una llamada telefónica.

One minute, I need to make a phone call.

Pedro: Bueno. Voy a tomar una siesta.

Ok. I'm going to take a nap.

Now Practice: hacer una llamada telefónica

Repeat Aloud 3 times slowly to practice

---

169. mandar un mensajito—sending a text

(NOTE: there are many different ways of saying this. "Mandar un mesnajito," is just one of the ways. You can also say, "enviar sms," or "mandar un text," or even using the verb, "textear." There are many ways to say it and there is no universally agreed upon correct way to say it, so just copy whatever the local people say.)

Dialogue:

Margarita: Dígame cuando llegas.

Let me know when you arrive.

Pedro: Claro. Te mandare un mensajito.

Of course. I'll send you a text.

Now Practice: mandar un mensajito

Repeat Aloud 3 times slowly to practice

---

170. hacer un viaje —take a trip

(NOTE: again, in Spanish they use the verb "Make," whereas in English, we'd say "take a trip," or "go on a trip.")

Dialogue:

Margarita: Quiero hacer un viaje.

I want to take a trip.

Pedro: ¿Sí? ¿Dónde quieres ir?

Yeah? Where do you want to go?

Now Practice: hacer un viaje

Repeat Aloud 3 times slowly to practice

171. tener prisa—to be in a hurry
(Note: this translates to, "To have a hurry." Most of the time in Spanish they use the verb "to have," or "avere," whereas, in English we'd say, "To be in a hurry.")

Dialogue:

Margarita: ¿Cuándo puedes hablar?

When can you talk?

Pedro: Ahora no. ¡Tengo prisa! Llego tarde al trabajo.

Not now. I'm in a hurry! I'm late for work.

Now Practice: tener prisa

Repeat Aloud 3 times slowly to practice

---

172. estar de mal humor—to be in a bad mood

Dialogue:

Margarita: ¿Qué pasa? ¿hay algo mal?

What's going on? Is something wrong?

Pedro: No sé. Tal vez solo estoy de mal humor.

I don't know. Maybe I'm just in a bad mood.

Now Practice: estar de mal humor

Repeat Aloud 3 times slowly to practice

---

173. Tener razón —to be right

(NOTE: this directly translates to, "to have reason." There's not really a more direct translation that would make sense, but it's the perfect way of telling someone they're right).

Dialogue:

Margarita: Debemos salir pronto. Hay mucho tráfico.

We should leave soon. There's a lot of traffic.

Pedro: Tienes razón. Vamos ahora.

You're right. Let's go now.

Now Practice: Tener razón

174. Estar equivocado—to be wrong

(Note: you can also use equivocarse to say that someone or something is wrong. To tell someone they're wrong, it's also correct to say, "te equivocas.")

Dialogue:

Margarita: Creo que te olvidaste que mi cumpleaños es el mes que viene.

I think you forgot that birthday is next month.

Pedro: Estas equivocado. ¡No lo olvide!

You're wrong. I did not forget it!

Now Practice: Estar equivocado

Repeat Aloud 3 times slowly to practice

175. Tener hambre—to be hungry

Dialogue:

Margarita: ¿Tienes hambre? Hice la cena.

Are you hungry? I made dinner.

Pedro: ¡Genial! Tengo mucho hambre.

Great! I'm very hungry.

Now Practice: tener hambre

Repeat Aloud 3 times slowly to practice

176. Estar cansado—to be tired

(NOTE: notice how here we use the verb "to be," instead of "to have" like many other situations. You can also say "tener sueno," for "to be sleepy," or you could also say "estar somnoliento," for, "to be drowsy.")

Dialogue:

Margarita: Te ves cansado.

You look tired.

Pedro: Si. Estoy muy cansado hoy.

Yes, I'm very tired today.

Now Practice: estar cansado

Repeat Aloud 3 times slowly to practice

---

177. irse—to leave

(NOTE: typically, you'll follow this phrase with a qualifier. For example, you could say "We need to leave soon," you could say: "Necesitamos irnos pronto.")

Dialogue:

Margarita: ¿Qué hora es?

What time is it?

Pedro: Casi las ocho. Tienes que irte en cinco minutos.

Almost eight. You have to leave in 5 minutes.

Now Practice: irse

Repeat Aloud 3 times slowly to practice

---

178. escribelo por favor—please write it down

Dialogue:

Margarita: Necesito que traigas algunas cosas de la tienda para mí.

I need you to get some things from the store for me.

Pedro: Escribelos, por favor, y yo los comprare.

Write them down please and I'll buy them.

Now Practice: escribelo por favor

Repeat Aloud 3 times slowly to practice

---

179. ¿Te gustaria bailar conmigo?—Would you like to dance with me?

(NOTE: you could also simply say, "Bailamos?" which translates to, "Let's dance?" or "Dance with me?")

Dialogue:

Margarita: ¡Me encanta esta canción!

I love this song!

Pedro: Entonces, ¿Te gustaría bailar conmigo?

Then would you like to dance with me?

Now Practice: ¿Te gustaria bailar conmigo?

Repeat Aloud 3 times slowly to practice

---

180. te extraño—I miss you

(NOTE: you could also say, "Te echo de menos," as another common way of telling someone you miss them.)

Dialogue:

Margarita: ¡Regrese! ¿Me extrañaste?

I'm back! Did you miss me?

Pedro: ¡Dar una buena acogida! ¿Como fue?

Welcome back! How was it?

Now Practice: te extraño

Repeat Aloud 3 times slowly to practice

---

181. Te amo—I love you

(NOTE: Saying, "te amo," is more of a serious or romantic "I love you," but to say more in fun to friends, you can use, "te quiero.")

Dialogue:

Margarita: Te amo, Pedro.

I love you, Pedro.

Pedro: Yo también te amo, Margarita.

I love you too, Margarita.

Now Practice: Te amo

Repeat Aloud 3 times slowly to practice

---

182. ¿Vienes aqui a menudo?—do you come here often?

Dialogue:

Margarita: ¿Te gusta esta taberna?

Do you like this bar?

Pedro: Si. ¿Vienes aquí a menudo?

Yes, do you come here often?

Now Practice: ¿Vienes aquí a menudo?

Repeat Aloud 3 times slowly to practice

---

183. Dejar solo—leave (me) alone

(NOTE: you could also say, "dejame en paz," which translates to "leave me in peace," or another way to say it is, "no me molestas," which is more like, "don't bother me.")

Dialogue:

Margarita: Ese hombre me sigue molestando.

That man keeps bothering me.

Pedro: se lo diré a él a dejarte solo.

I'll tell him to leave you alone.

Now Practice: Dejar solo

Repeat Aloud 3 times slowly to practice

---

184. Lo intentaré más tarde—I'll try again later

(NOTE: this translates to "I'll try it later." For more emphasis you can say, "Lo intentaré de nuevo más tarde," which means, "I'll try again later."

Dialogue:

Margarita: ¿Hablaste con tu mama?

Did you talk to your mom?

Pedro: Ella no contestó el teléfono. Lo intentaré más tarde.

She didn't answer the phone. I'll try again later.

Now Practice: Lo intentaré más tarde

Repeat Aloud 3 times slowly to practice

---

185. No puedo esperar—I can't wait to…

(NOTE: use this to express your excitement about something.)

Dialogue:

Margarita: No puedo esperar a terminar trabajo.

I can't wait to finish work.

Pedro: Yo Tambien. Ha sido un largo día.

Me too. It's been a long day.

Now Practice: No puedo esperar

Repeat Aloud 3 times slowly to practice

---

186. Me hace la boca agua—My mouth is watering

(NOTE: this directly translates to something like, "it makes my mouth water" Delicious Hispanic food may cause you to use this phrase quite often.)

Dialogue:

Margarita: Puedo oler las palomitas

I can smell the popcorn.

Pedro: ¡Yo sé! Me hace la boca agua.

I know. It's making my mouth water.

Now Practice: Me hace la boca agua.

Repeat Aloud 3 times slowly to practice

---

187. ¡Qué vergüenza!—Shame on you!

(Note, this translates more to, "what a shame," but it's implied that it's someone's fault as in, "shame on you." For more emphasis, you can say: "¡Deberías darte vergüenza!" which means, "you should be ashamed." When it's no one's fault and you just want to remark that something is "a shame," or "a pity," you can say: "¡Que lastima!")

Dialogue:

Margarita: No esperé para ti para comer.

I did not wait for you to eat.

Pedro: ¡Qué vergüenza!

Shame on you!

Now Practice: ¡Qué vergüenza!

188. desahogarse—Blow off steam,

(NOTE: in Spanish they actually have a concise verb for this. It's very efficient. The closest English verb would be, "to unburden," but it's used like, "to blow off steam.")

Dialogue:

Margarita: Necesito desahogarme.

I need to blow off steam.

Pedro: Entonces vamos al gimnasio juntos.

Then let's go to the gym together.

Now Practice: desahogarse

Repeat Aloud 3 times slowly to practice

189. dar el beneficio de la duda—Give the benefit of the doubt

Dialogue:

Margarita: ¡Mi jefe olvido nuestro encuentro de nuevo!

My boss forgot our meeting again!

Pedro: Dale el beneficio de la duda.

Give him the benefit of the doubt.

Now Practice: dar el beneficio de la duda

Repeat Aloud 3 times slowly to practice

190. No juzgues un libro por su portada—don't judge a book by it's cover

Dialogue:

Margarita: Este restaurante no parece bueno.

This restaurant doesn't look good.

Pedro: No juzgues un libro por su portada

Give him the benefit of the doubt.

Now Practice: No juzgues un libro por su portada

Repeat Aloud 3 times slowly to practice

191. dedos cruzados —fingers crossed

(NOTE: if you want to say, "keep your fingers crossed," you can say: "Mantén tus dedos cruzados.")

Dialogue:

Margarita: Compré un billete de loteria.

I bought a lottery ticket.

Pedro: ¡Buena suerte! Mantén tus dedos cruzados.

Good luck! Keep your fingers crossed.

Now Practice: dedos cruzados

Repeat Aloud 3 times slowly to practice

---

192. ¡Qué lata!—what a pain

(NOTE: there are a few different ways of saying this, "que lata," is more like, "how annoying!" or "what a bore!" You could also say, "¡qué suplicio!" which means something like, "What an ordeal!")

Dialogue:

Margarita: ¡Olvide mi celular en el taxi!

I forgot my phone in the taxi!

Pedro: ¡Que lata! Llamamos la compañía.

What a pain! Let's call the company.

Now Practice: ¡Qué lata!

Repeat Aloud 3 times slowly to practice

---

193. No tener pelos en la lengua--Tell it to me straight

(Note: This translates directly to "not to have hairs on the tongue." This is a colorful Spanish idiom that is useful when you want someone to "tell it like it is" or be "straight forward with you."

Dialogue:

Margarita: Tengo mala noticias...

I have bad news.

Pedro: ¿Que paso? No tenga pelos en la lengua.

What happened? Tell it to me straight.

Now Practice: No tener pelos en la lengua

Repeat Aloud 3 times slowly to practice

---

194. ¡Estoy muy ilusionado!--I'm very excited!

(NOTE: you can also say, "¡Tengo mucha ilusión! These are more casual ways of saying it. You may also hear, ¡Estoy muy emocionado! Which is the more formal word for "excited.")

Dialogue:

Margarita: ¿Listo para el show?

Are you ready for the show?

Pedro: ¡Si! ¡Estoy muy ilusionado de verlo!

Yes! I'm very excited to see it!

Now Practice: ¡Estoy muy ilusionado!

Repeat Aloud 3 times slowly to practice

---

195. ¿Puedo echar un vistazo?—Can I take a look?

(NOTE: this directly translates to something like, "Can I throw a glance?" It's a casual and colloquial way of asking someone if you can take a look at something. "Podria tomar una mirada," is the more formal way of saying it that is less common with native speakers.)

Dialogue:

Margarita: Creo que la TV está rota.

I think the TV is broken.

Pedro: ¿Puedo echar un vistazo?

Can I take a look at it?

Now Practice: ¿Puedo echar un vistazo?

Repeat Aloud 3 times slowly to practice

---

196. Un rollo—boring

(NOTE: this is a common idiomatic way of saying something is boring, "es un rollo..." similar to the English expression "a bore." The conventional way of saying it that you probably learned in school is "es aburrido.")

Dialogue:

Margarita: ¿Como fue la película?

How was the movie?

Pedro: No bueno. Fue un rollo.

Not Good. It was so boring.

Now Practice: un rollo

Repeat Aloud 3 times slowly to practice

---

197. Venga hombre!—No way!/Come on

(NOTE: while this directly translates to, "Come man," it is similar to the English expression, "come on" or "come on man." This is something we say when someone is being ridiculous or when we don't believe something)

Dialogue:

Pedro: No puedo compartir esta pizza contigo.

I can't share this pizza with you.

Margarita: ¡Venga hombre! Tienes mucha, puedes compartir.

Come on! You have a lot, you can share.

Now Practice: Venga hombre!

Repeat Aloud 3 times slowly to practice

---

198. ¡Tienes toda de la razón del mundo!—You're absolutely right!

Dialogue:

Pedro: Creo que tu jefe llegara tarde otra vez.

I think your boss will be late again.

Margarita: Tienes toda de la razón del mundo. Lo creo también.

You're absolutely right. I think so too.

Now Practice: ¡Tienes toda de la razón del mundo!

199. Perder los estribos—to lose your temper

Dialogue:

Pedro: El tráfico es muy mal. ¡Lo odio!

The traffic is so bad! I hate it!

Margarita: Cálmate. No pierdas los estribos.

Calm down. Don't lose your temper.

Now Practice: Perder los estribos

Repeat Aloud 3 times slowly to practice

200. Como ningun otro—unique/like no other

(NOTE: although you can use the word "unico," for unique. Saying "como ningun otro," is a more colorful and sophisticated way to express the same thing.)

Dialogue:

Pedro: ¿Qué piensas de mi amigo Ramon?

What do you think of my friend Ramon?

Margarita: Creo que él es como ningún otro.

I think he is like no other.

Now Practice: como ningun otro

Repeat Aloud 3 times slowly to practice

We hope you've learned a lot from this book and we hope you now feel much more comfortable engaging in conversations with Spanish speakers. Mastering a language takes time and requires a lot of effort and commitment. Committing to working through books like this is a great way to accelerate your learning, but nothing can substitute the value of conversing in Spanish. Go on vacation to Mexico, or find a friend or family member that is also trying to learn Spanish. A useful challenge and exercise can be committing to communicating with someone in Spanish only. This means via text, when you're talking etc. It can be very difficult, but it will force you to start thinking in Spanish and applying what you learn. Language theory, and vocabulary can only take you so far.

Once you start having conversations, you'll grow more rapidly than ever before. You'll get more comfortable with the language and develop more of an intuitive sense about it. Before long, you'll know what to say without even thinking about it, and you'll be able to understand people without having to revert to English. Using phrases like those you've learned in this book will help you call to mind the appropriate things to say in conversation, and don't be afraid to use the phrase, "Que quieres decir con…." Or "que significa" when someone says something you don't understand. Also, the phrase "como se dice…" will help you out when you can't think of the word or phrase you want to say.

We wish you all the best of luck on your language journey. Gracias para leer este libro. Si te gusto que has leído, por favor dejar un comentario para nosotros.

Adiós por ahora.

Made in the USA
Las Vegas, NV
31 October 2022

58526326R00080